Keighley Campus Leeds City College
Tel: 01535 685010

# Coming of Age

Celebrating **21** Years of Mela in the UK

**The Caste Folk Musicians of Rajasthan performing traditional folk music on stage in Lister Park**
Bradford Mela | 1997 | © Tim Smith

**Team:**

| | |
|---|---|
| Project Coordinator | Mandeep Samra |
| Curator | David Schischka Thomas |
| Production & Advisory Team | Ben Pugh, Skinder Hundal, Champak Kumar and Bhavesh Jani |
| Researchers | Roshni Belakavadi, Tom Hodgson, Shabana Kausar, Pavan Sembi and Lu Li |
| Finance Administrator | Amy Law |

**'Coming of Age' book:**

| | |
|---|---|
| Writer | Irna Qureshi |
| Editor | Steve Dearden |
| Photographers | Tim Smith, Nadeem Haider/APNA Arts, Alan Lodge, Bartosz Kali, Jagdish Patel/Frontline Images, Ashok Mistry and ArtReach |
| Designer | Harmeet Sembi (AIC.H) |
| Printer | CSM (Complete Service Management), Bradford |

**'Coming of Age' exhibition:**

This book is accompanied by a photographic touring exhibition which will travel to the following two venues:

**New Art Exchange, Nottingham, 29 May – 24 July 2010**
**Cartwright Hall Art Gallery, Bradford, 7 August – 7 November 2010**

To book the exhibition and for further information on the exhibition tour please visit: **www.mela21.co.uk**

ISBN: 978-0-946657-63-6

This project has been kindly supported by:

Principal sponsor and regular supporter of Bradford Mela:

# Contents

**Coming of Age** | Celebrating 21 Years of Mela in the UK

# Foreword

Under a massive tensile structure, amazing dancers spin, with aerial performers suspended above; the scent from freshly piped jalebies wafts past and in the distance, there is the sound of a qawwali. Entering from the massive temporary car park, a group of young women work their spectacularly styled hair, clothes and nails. There are few places in the world where such a blend of sensations - of high and popular art, of food, army and council promotional stalls - can exist in the same place. The mela is a space where the social, cultural and political agendas of the past twenty years have collided together, by stealth, and with impact. In *Coming of Age*, melas are identified as a truly open form of celebration unbound by rules of form, social class or race. Here, all types of creativity mingle - food, music, cars, fashion and design - in a way that is accessible for many, and beyond the constraints of our class loaded society. Melas have been popular, engaging and far reaching, yet until now - despite their wide audience drawn from multiple UK communities - critically invisible. This book carefully describes their political roots, growth and success and reflects the shifts from local to international agendas.

The content of a British mela is implicitly anti-racist drawing in multiple, diverse and intergenerational communities with different rhythms that appeal to families, youth and indeed specific faith groups within a shared atmosphere of celebration. The perception of the Asian community as closed, impenetrable and obscure is debunked. Visit any mela in the UK and it is clear that this is simply not the case. They simultaneously offer a sense of family and an open welcome. There is real power in the cultural displays and multiple entry points, from plates of food to transcendent beats and visual displays.

*Coming of Age* tracks the creation and success of the mela, showing how melas have been sensitive to geography and spread, and shaped by local people and agendas, and their communities. Melas reflect their locality with different tones and textures, and from Scotland to London artists have seen these spaces as a chance to experiment, develop and share their work. The book describes how young artists have used melas to forge their practice, and how mid and mature artists are recognised. It also maps the intriguing outward web of mela relationships to community radio, national broadcast, and online media.

It is a joy to see the many unsung activists, entrepreneurs and creative thinkers that have shaped the mela form finally given the credit and recognition that they richly deserve within the pages of this fascinating and long overdue publication.

**Keith Khan, Artist**

**Coming of Age** | Celebrating 21 Years of Mela in the UK

# Coming of Age

Celebrating **21** Years of Mela in the UK

# Inventing the Mela

Melas have been held in the Indian subcontinent for thousands of years but they are a relatively recent phenomenon in Britain. The term *mela* stems from the Sanskrit word *gathering* and is used to describe all manner of cultural and religious celebrations. In Britain the term encompasses the earliest bazaars, fairs, family days and festivals organised by the South Asian diaspora. These were celebratory events, usually held outdoors, probably free of charge, and attracted the entire family. Skinder Hundal, one of the directors of Nottingham Mela, explains that the purpose of the earliest melas was to reconnect the first generation of migrants with their South Asian roots: *"The whole romantic dream of the mela was to have the kambal (blanket) out on the grass, the paranthas, the achar (pickle), the raita, and share in a festival environment, with street performers or performers on stage. It was that notion of what happened in India and Pakistan being brought over here, because that was a gap in people's experiences, and the second generation of Asians were detached from that experience. So it was connecting the parents with their experiences of back home, recreating an element of that and then redefining it with the new generation here."*

Josie Singh performing classic Bollywood dance on the Lister Park lake | Bradford Mela | 1992 © Tim Smith

South Asian communities have held celebratory cultural events in Britain for many years. This book concentrates on the development of two of the country's most established and innovative melas, Bradford and Nottingham. They first took place within three weeks of each other during the summer of 1988 and have defined the annual summer event as a national institution. While their journeys started together, Nottingham and Bradford Melas have taken different paths. Twenty-one years later, Bradford has emerged as one of Europe's largest multi arts festival attracting audiences of over 200,000. Nottingham Mela is a more modest festival attracting up to 20,000 people, but prepared the ground for a new £5m flagship contemporary arts centre, which showcases visual and performing arts on an international and culturally diverse level.

This book is based on a series of conversations with mela organisers and programmers, artists, musicians, cultural commentators and stakeholders. It places Nottingham and Bradford Melas within a national mela landscape and celebrates some of their achievements. It uses extracts from the conversations to highlight the breadth of artforms that make up Bradford and Nottingham Melas, to consider the artistic challenges in presenting cutting edge work in these environments, and to demonstrate mela's commitment to developing the arts.

Some of the earliest melas in Britain were based on faith – marking religious festivals such as Baisakhi, Diwali and Eid - and didn't necessarily promote dialogue outside a particular community. These gatherings were held at venues like Indian or Pakistani community centres, or places of worship, which were perceived to belong to a particular faith or community. This is precisely what made Nottingham and Bradford Melas unique; they were as much about the Asian community taking ownership as they were about creating an opportunity for dialogue with other communities. This happened because Bradford and Nottingham Melas were held on sites that were neutral and therefore inclusive. Skinder Hundal believes that the melas held in 1988 were groundbreaking because they provided one of the first opportunities for a celebration in a public sphere which encouraged participation from different communities: *"The communities were taking ownership of their own destiny in promoting the arts and culture and making sure there was something there for the communities to enjoy and be proud of. There were only the day-timers, or the commercial shows, but there wasn't a collective space where all the communities came together, of all Asian origins – the Pakistani, Indian, Bangladeshi, Sri Lankan - that was the point of the mela. It was a connecting point for all the South Asian communities to come together as a creative voice."*

Bradford photojournalist Tim Smith has photographed almost every Bradford Mela in its twenty-one year history. He remembers that the first Bradford Mela offered the British an introduction to Asian culture in a way that was accessible: *"It was difficult to get the mainstream press in London interested in events held by and for the Asian community, no matter how big they were. It was too foreign for them. It was like, 'Eid? What's that got to do with us?' It was almost like you had to ring up the religious affairs correspondent! But if you said, 'There's 50,000 people singing and dancing in a public space in Bradford', then that's a whole new ball game really. It was almost like bringing the Asian community out of the closet. So the Mela was like a slab of Asian culture that had been picked up from the subcontinent and put in a public park in Bradford, and that's what made it interesting to newspaper editors. They felt they could cover the Mela because they felt it had some relevance for their readership. You know, music and dance and food was something they could grasp."*

Naseem Khan, arts policy advisor and a previous Head of Diversity at Arts Council England, explains that the dawn of large scale cultural melas like Bradford and Nottingham in 1988, coincided with the emergence of an Asian youth scene in Britain. Melas quickly became the place to be seen, and the place to showcase popular Asian culture. *"It was very impressive actually - hundreds and hundreds of Asian people together - and that sense of obvious strength and 'solidarity' and a sense of power, if only economic power. And the creative voice was actually quite affirmative at that early stage. Not only were the Asian arts actually coming out into the mainstream but you also have the shift in the playground. If you remember way back, the idea of Asian kids was of being wimpy compared to black kids, and not being sexy and not having any kind of desirable image, and the whole thing of Paki bashing. The mela actually perhaps had a hand in showing the community back to itself, reflecting a sense of numerical power and creative vibrancy. To actually see something which was writ large across the face of society made you feel good.*

*It was the sense of this being normality as opposed to being marginality."*

Yasmin Nazir was a teenage volunteer with Apna Arts, whose volunteers were pivotal to shaping the Nottingham Mela. The ethos of Apna Arts as well as the earliest melas in Nottingham was to advance Asian arts, particularly within the youth to give them a stronger sense of themselves: *"What we didn't have at the time was any role models to look up to, you know positive role models. And here we were, surrounded by local, national artists and then international artists who were at the peak of their success, and then there were others who were riding that success and they were Asian. To me, it gave me that sense that I could actually achieve what I wanted to do, because here in front of me were people who'd managed to do that. They'd overcome barriers and transcended those divisions, and crossed over into mainstream western music charts and stuff. So it was that sense of pride, a sense of identity, a sense of grounding, like 'Yeah, I know who I am; I know where I come from and I actually feel comfortable and proud of my roots.'"*

The Channi-Upuli Dance Ensemble from Sri Lanka performing a spectacular choreographed journey through the art and history of Sri Lankan heritage | Bradford Mela | 1998 | © Tim Smith

# Bradford Mela

The story of Bradford Mela is inextricably linked to Bradford Festival which was conceived a year before Bradford Mela in 1987. Inspired by the success of a local festival created to reinvigorate the Little Germany area of Bradford, the local authority's Economic Development Unit invited the organiser to create a festival for the entire city. That organiser, Allan Brack, was a former art gallery curator, who had been introduced to Dusty Rhodes, an artist-cum-outdoor-staging specialist, by a local art college lecturer. As Dusty Rhodes explains, the idea of what the festival could be was strongly influenced by their involvement in the local peace movement: *"We'd both been campaigners against racism and fascism and in a way, doing the Festival and then the Mela was a continuation of how we saw the city politically and what the threats to the city were - the constant fascist threat, not just the organised fascism but also the low level racism. We lived through a period where black and Asian people on the streets of Bradford were being physically attacked."*

Bradford College, where Champak Kumar was a student, was also a focus of anti-racist campaigns. As part of his role as Secretary of the Indian Society, Champak began to programme small-scale music events for students. He established Oriental Arts, one of the country's oldest Asian arts organisations, in 1976. The same year, a number of students from the College and University formed the Bradford Asian Youth Movement, to challenge the growing threat of racism and activities of the National Front. The main force behind Apna Arts and Nottingham Mela, Parbinder Singh, was a student at Bradford University at the same time. Champak and Parbinder became members of the Asian Youth Movement, and Champak organised fundraisers for their cause.

Oriental Arts' focus on local artistic development emerged organically in its early years, after Champak realised there were no South Asian singers, dancers or performers available to participate in a variety show he was planning. Determined to showcase local Asian talent at the upcoming event, Champak acted as a mentor putting musicians and dancers in touch with one another; helping with choreography and costumes; and encouraging them to rehearse regularly. *"The aim of Oriental Arts was to promote South Asian arts, giving opportunities to the communities. So people came and said, 'Look, I'm a dholak player', 'I'm a vocalist', so we got this talent together."* This is how Nachda Punjab, Bradford's oldest traditional bhangra dance troupe was formed. A tabla and dholak player himself, Champak also formed a group, Naya Saaz, which performed covers of classic Bollywood film songs. Many of these acts performed at the first Mela, and some reformed specifically to perform as part of Bradford Mela's 21st year celebrations.

Oriental Arts had already gained a reputation for programming multicultural festivals when it was invited to programme South Asian artists for Bradford Festival. The first Bradford Festival ran from 17th to 27th September 1987 and established the formula for a community led, multi arts festival. Plans became more ambitious the following year. To complement the street arts festival, a finale was planned in Manningham's Lister Park, as well as a standalone event to honour Bradford's Asian communities. Champak Kumar remembers being approached with the idea: *"They said, 'We want to do a huge outdoor event. What could it be?' And of course I said, 'A mela!' When people in India and Pakistan celebrate Diwali or Baisakhi or Eid, they always call it a mela. And I used to see a lot Bollywood films, and when they mentioned a mela in the films, you would see a fair, you would see colours, and you would see artists dancing in the films, and I thought mela is the key word to use."*

The first Bradford Mela was held on Shearbridge Road Playing Fields near the University on 18th September 1988 attracting a 10,000 strong crowd. The first Bradford Mela was so successful that organisers decided to relocate it the following year to Lister Park, where it would form part of the Festival Finale weekend. Dusty Rhodes explains that while the mela had its roots in the Indian subcontinent, the event in Bradford was a gathering for everybody. *"We made a decision to give the Bradford Mela pride of place as the Festival Finale on the Sunday. We were thinking what we ought to do is make the Sunday the*

*Festival Finale and honour a different community in Bradford every year. It'll be the Asian community this year with the Mela, then it'll be the Poles or the Ukrainians or a Caribbean finale."* But fusing the two together meant the event grew and the boundary between the Mela and the Festival Finale began to blur.

The Bradford Festival mobilised the entire city into making the event happen. The guiding principle was less about attracting renowned artists and more about city-wide participation, and encouraging different sections of the community to collaborate. Oriental Arts established a Mela Steering Group, appointing community worker Gurpaul Sandhu as the chairperson, to bring together representatives of different South Asian communities, and to garner support from groups like the Bangladeshi Youth Organisation and local businesses. Local art college students converged on Lister Park to help build structures and stages for the event. Dusty Rhodes, one of the Festival Directors, says the artistic vision was one of community ownership and celebration. *"It was a giant artslab of fellow travellers doing these things together. We used to go into the park a week or two before the event and start building the thing, and people that we didn't even know would come with huge tubs of curry and feed us because we were working to build the Mela. These were spontaneous gestures. There was just a real sense that the event was by and for the community, and anybody who had an idea could come along and join in."*

The two week Bradford Festival became a multi arts, multicultural celebration including music, dance, visual arts, theatre, cabaret, film and poetry. One of the outstanding features of the Festival was the wide range of street entertainments. There were also events in local parks, schools programmes, community programmes as well as a Lord Mayor's Festival Parade. These events were rounded off with the Festival Finale and Mela, amid fireworks and a theatrical extravaganza on a specially erected Stage on the Lake in Lister Park. The Festival team included a schools officer and an elderly people's officer whose job was to encourage participation in arts workshops which could feed into local parks events. To facilitate this level of activity, artists were booked to perform in a series of events throughout the Festival. Local acrobatic theatre troupe, Skinning the Cat, performed in the Bradford Festival and Mela on many occasions. Their involvement varied year to year. One year the troupe toured five different parks within a week and then performed at the Mela. Trapeze artist Becky Truman realised that the Festival's peripheral programmes were about taking the Festival out into the community: *"The touring parks took you to places in Bradford where no one else normally went – you know little parks and different communities, people that might not necessarily make it to the Mela. The areas were picked because things didn't normally go there, I think."* Not only did the central pool of artists enhance each event's offer, but this mutual dependence also made financial sense, as Mark Fielding, Festival Director from 1997-2000 explains: *"If you've got an act from Spain, you don't just want to bring them for the day. It would cost a fortune so we'd put them in the street, we'd put them in the Mela, we'd take them to local park events. We'd put* them in some schools because they might want to run some workshops, or we might put on a special event just for them, depending on what it was."

In 2002, just as the city was gearing up to bid as Capital of Culture 2008, Bradford Council assigned the running of Bradford Festival and the Mela to a different company. Sheena Wrigley, Head of Bradford Theatres, Arts and Festivals (2003-2007) considers the rationale for this decision: *"One of the reasons why they were brought in was to create a more professionalised and a more impactful Mela Festival in the hope it could form a major part of the 2008 Capital of Culture bid."* Paul Brookes, who led Bradford's bid, regarded the Mela as an asset to positively position Bradford as a culturally diverse city: *"The Mela was most certainly seen as a demonstration of something that brought together communities in a celebratory way. 'Europe's biggest and best Mela' is how we described it. That multiculturalism that the Mela represents, the way the Mela was a symbol of some of that multiculturalism, was absolutely at the centre of the bid."*

Liverpool won the Capital of Culture bid. Meanwhile, the outsourcing of Bradford Festival and Mela changed the event completely. The Mela became a glossy, high profile pop festival with a strong emphasis on bhangra which attracted the young but alienated many others. The new event disregarded the relationships which had been crafted over fifteen years of Festival and Mela in Bradford. Community groups, artists, families all felt ignored and the situation created ill ease. Jenny Wilson, who was working on the Festival as a Freelance Consultant and Producer at that time, explains what went wrong: *"They weren't from Bradford and weren't connected into the communities. And because the old Festival had been deconstructed and destroyed, then all the relationships and goodwill that had grown up over a lot of years had gone with that, so actually they had an impossible job trying to make a mela happen from that place. And their understanding of the Mela wasn't about growing up out of the community from the grassroots because they were coming in to produce something with an international view. The old Festival had a homespun quality to it, and City of Culture didn't think this would win it. In fact they destroyed its uniqueness, the very thing that made it attractive."*

In 2004, when the Local Authority stepped in as the custodians of the Bradford Mela, organisers made efforts to broaden the Mela's appeal and audience, and tried to recapture some of its old personality. Two years later, the Festival and Mela became separated for the first time. Bradford Council took the decision to fold the Festival in 2007, leaving the way clear for Bradford Mela to become the main cultural offer in the city's annual calendar.

**Mela Punjab Da recreating a typical fairground scene from the Punjab at Bradford's first ever Mela**
Bradford Mela | 1988 | © Tim Smith

**Triveni Dance Troupe** | Nottingham Mela | 1991 | © Nadeem Haider/APNA Arts

# Nottingham Mela

The visionary behind Nottingham Mela, Parbinder Singh, studied at Bradford University where he too became involved in Bradford's peace movement. Parbinder returned to Nottingham to become a youth worker and set about creating opportunities to empower Asian youth. After clashing with exclusivist community centres that discouraged different Asian communities from mixing, Parbinder established the Ekta Youth Group – Ekta meaning oneness or unity - which was open to everyone, irrespective of ethnicity or faith. A few years later, with friend Resham Aujla, Parbinder returned to his community arts roots to establish Apna Arts (Our Arts). This was a part time and unpaid venture for Parbinder, set up specifically to empower the young people in his charge as a youth worker. Apna Arts aimed to advance Asian arts, especially within the youth; to use the arts to bring together different sections of the community; and to stimulate arts employment and training facilities. Parbinder began to mobilise the Asian youth, uniting them to organise fundraising events for a number of high profile deportation cases.

**APNA Arts Volunteers, Parbinder Singh and Gurinder Chada** | Newham Mela | 1993 | © Nadeem Haider/APNA Arts

**Apna Sangeet** | Nottingham Mela | 1991 | © Nadeem Haider/APNA Arts

Apna Arts developed into a vibrant organisation, winning awards for its work with young volunteers, many of whom were students from the city's two universities. One of the volunteers was Nadeem Haider whose interest in photography led him to Apna Arts. He believes the organisation helped him to rediscover the heritage he had rejected as a result of experiencing racism as a teenager: *"The National Front was in its heyday and I remember going to school through the woods because there'd be Paki bashing going on. I remember one of the sports teachers saying he is going down South because there's too many blacks and Pakis here and he can't be doing with it. You were just made to feel unwanted. I'd grown up with this negativity through racism attached to my culture and I think there was this reluctance to express your cultural heritage naturally. There was all this, you know 'keeping quiet' about it. It was quite a reserved and inward way of living. It was a form of denial, I guess. So if you can imagine having experienced that for ten years and then coming back into Apna Arts and through the Mela, it was just like a 'born again' type of feeling. People felt at ease and open about themselves. I felt there was a sense of belonging there and the word Apna itself obviously has that connection. This was a chance to big yourself up, to be able to celebrate yourself and your cultural heritage and be proud of it, and that's how I was attracted to the organisation."*

Yasmin Nazir had been a member of the Ekta Youth Group for many years before becoming an Apna Arts volunteer. *"Our parents didn't actually understand that we were a product of two totally different cultures, and we somehow had to learn to manage those two competing aspects. And there was nowhere for us to vent our frustration or seek some support. And that was the beauty of Ekta and Apna where we actually came together and it was almost like a support vehicle for all of us. Through each other we gained a sense of our own identity and we gained a sense of belonging."*

Before long, Apna Arts was working with a team of forty Asian and non-Asian volunteers, the majority of whom were in their late teens. The organisation was keen to accommodate their interests. Thus, it was the volunteers who came up with the idea to hold a National Festival of Asian Arts and Music in Nottingham. The concept was a ticketed, two day national festival, showcasing a range of South Asian artforms. Although Parbinder and Resham took the lead, the ideas, planning and organisation came from the volunteers. They were involved at every level from giving publicity interviews and marketing, to selecting artists and tracking them down. Yasmin was nineteen when she got involved in planning the event: *"There was an upcoming artist at the time, Johnny Zee, and a lot of the volunteers really wanted Johnny Zee to come and perform. And Parbinder said, 'If you can convince him to come and perform I have no problems'. So that's how some of the artists came about. The bhangra artists were really easy to get hold of because there were bhangra do's all over the country. You just went to a bhangra do and you approached the artist. The hardest band was Alaap simply because they were internationally renowned. We didn't have internet in those days, so it was a question of tracking them down through record sleeves, and talking to people at the record company, getting them to pass messages on, and then finally getting a call from their agent. So it took us weeks to make contact with Alaap but persuading them to perform in the Festival was really easy."*

The event was renamed Melton Medes Festival of Asian Arts and Music after a three year sponsorship deal was struck with a local business. Owned by Indian entrepreneur Nat Puri, now one of Britain's richest Asians, the Melton Medes Group is a Nottingham based, multi million pound manufacturing and engineering empire. With sponsorship in place, dates for the ambitious festival were fixed for the second weekend of August 1988. An Asian arts festival on this scale was so rare that Apna Arts received letters of support from Margaret Thatcher and Neil Kinnock which were published in the souvenir programme. Saturday was promoted as Bhangra Heatwave aimed at the youth market. The Sunday was dedicated to classical music and arts and promoted as Sangeet Ka Mela (Music Festival), and aimed to draw a family audience. The volunteers embarked on a national marketing campaign, handing out promotional flyers and badges at bhangra gigs, WOMAD and Bradford Mela. Flyers were posted to mosques, gurdwaras and youth organisations throughout the country. This level of intensive experience helped the volunteers to build skills and stimulated some to pursue careers in the arts. Volunteer Nadeem Haider eventually became an Apna Arts employee: *"Come April, May time, all the young kids just used to gather and take over the building when they started to plan for the Mela. There were Hindus, Sikhs, Gujaratis and Bengalis, it was so mixed it was incredible. At that time it was unique I thought - to plan for*

*the Mela - because it was all volunteer led. They used to come and plan whatever they wanted to do, either the publicity or the fashion shows. It was so close knit and it was providing a unique opportunity for the young people to be trained in all sorts of different things from stage management to marketing. And there were people like myself who had no qualifications so I stayed on as a volunteer and then eventually I was employed by Apna Arts as an administrator. This organisation grew and these young people were given this opportunity to grow alongside the organisation and the Mela."*

In 1994, Apna Arts began to concentrate on year round development work instead of focussing purely on one festival – a necessary move if the organisation was to build a potential audience and develop the skills of its volunteers. In 2004, Apna Arts and its sister organisation EMACA (East Midlands African Caribbean Arts), secured funding to build a £5.5m art centre dedicated to developing and showcasing contemporary visual art practice from the African, Caribbean and South Asian diasporas. In 2005, Apna Arts and EMACA merged into one organisation, The New Art Exchange. Nottingham Mela did not take place for three years (2001-2003), allowing Apna Arts to concentrate on its year round development. During this period, new community partnerships were also solidified, for instance with South Asian arts umbrella organisation Nottingham Asian Arts Council (NAAC), which now acts as partner in the running of Nottingham Mela. An important part of the new model was to form the Nottingham Mela Support Group, comprising of key community members and organisations, to help deliver the Mela.

Several Apna Arts volunteers now form part of the New Art Exchange team including: Mohan Khera who became a Director of Apna Arts and is now a Director of the New Art Exchange; Chief Executive Skinder Hundal; Senior Curator David Thomas; and New Art Exchange Board Member Sukhy Johal MBE.

Nottingham Mela returned after the break as a smaller mela in a new venue, and has gone on to reinvent itself several times, according to the resources available. The 21st Nottingham Mela in 2009 took place as part of the city council's events programme, which enabled the Mela to share infrastructure costs. The core of the Mela is now located in Market Square in the city centre, attracting oblivious weekend shoppers as well as seasoned mela fans from further afield. Events were programmed in partnership with other venues like Theatre Royal, Nottingham Playhouse and also at the New Art Exchange, giving Nottingham Mela the feel of a fringe festival.

In keeping with the Mela's experimental nature, the dates for the 2009 event were strategically fixed to tie in with the Cricket World Twenty20 Cup which took place at Nottingham Trent Bridge. Skinder Hundal saw this as an unmissable marketing opportunity: *"On that weekend we had India, Bangladesh, Sri Lanka, Australia, in Nottingham. Because international news was covering the world cup cricket, they caught onto the fact that we've also got a mela happening - and South Asian culture, South Asian cricket teams, big teams, big audiences - there's a relationship there. So we got featured on international news, and in things like the Indian Times. That put Nottingham on the map*

*with the readers of India: 'Oh yes, Robin Hood! And they also do a mela! Amazing!' What was also amazing was that we had the Indian cricket team dancing at the back of Jazzy B's performance and we had the Australian Captain Ricky Ponting, with three or four of his team at the Mela ground. It's those kinds of stories that put a smile on my face because it's connected sport and culture together, and it's connected international locations. They may be small stories but they are still part of the jigsaw that symbolises modern Britain in a way which relates to the wider world and to some of the fastest growing economies. And that makes the Mela very relevant."*

**Jazzy B** | Nottingham Mela | 2009 | © Bartosz Kali

# Vision

## Community Ownership

Bradford Mela Producer Ben Pugh believes that a mela should be representative of the things that the community want to celebrate. For him, the most interesting melas are those doing something unique within their specific local context – the idea of showcasing something home grown on home ground. *"So much of what is key to mela is what's generated locally. It's the ideas and the collaboration and the passion of people on the ground that makes for the interesting mix. The demographic makeup in Liverpool or Edinburgh is completely different to how it is in Bradford, and when you go and see their melas, you can tell. So what you're looking at is different cultures showcasing their work in different ways, but showcasing them in a common format which is this idea of festival coming together in a park."*

Ben Pugh reveals that the 2009 Bradford Mela was the collaborative effort of 2,500 participants ranging from artists, core staff teams to litter pickers, security guards and community groups – a critical mass which contributes to the USP of Bradford Mela.

**Young men in Peel Park**   Bradford Mela   2009   © Tim Smith

*"You could deliver Bradford Mela with 200 people if you wanted but it would be a different event. The point is that the process and the involvement and the ownership are as important as what's being delivered. How we're doing it is as important as what we're doing, so the fact that there are 2,500 people represents an enormous critical mass of commitment and enthusiasm and support for the Mela that we could never pay for!"*

Nottingham and Bradford Melas are programmed by teams of highly skilled arts specialists. Gideon Seymour, Director of Fabric – Bradford's arts development agency - regards programming as a collaboration between the Mela team and the community. *"The Mela needs to be fed by a community that is conscious of and committed to and involved in developing the Mela. So the Mela needs to be not just about a small group of people saying, 'Who can we get this year?' But it's actually about a conversation - let people know what's there, or let people suggest what they want to see. A conversation like the old Festival used to do through word of mouth and sitting in smoke filled pubs."* One of the youngest melas in the country uses social networking sites to develop a conversation with its local community. Imran Iqbal founded Cardiff Multicultural Mela in 2007 in his home city after spending years visiting Slough Mela. By Imran's own admission, Cardiff Multicultural Mela replicates the stage, stalls and workshops format of many melas. Nevertheless, a sense of conversation with the local community is vital to ensuring their limited budget is spent as democratically as possible. *"We set up different Facebook Mela groups where we ask people, 'Who do you want to see at Cardiff Mela this*

*year?' We knew that H-Dhami was headlining lots of events last year and there was a unanimous demand for him, and we listened to that. We just had the budget to pay for one artist so H–Dhami is what we went for."*

Melas also act as unique spaces for communities to make connections with different aspects of their city. Skinder Hundal, who leads the programming team of Nottingham Mela, describes the event as *"an all embracing audience development framework"*. This is precisely why public service organisations use mela as a tool to engage audiences that have historically been difficult to reach. In 2009, the Bradford Mela organisers were approached by Friends of the Earth and the Anthony Nolan Trust. The organisations were interested in not merely using the Mela as an information point, but using the Mela to build meaningful relationships with local people. Out of this partnership grew a series of community zones on themes ranging from health, well being, environment to fair-trade, housed in enormous tents within the Mela site. Take up was high, with around fifteen local organisations being represented in the health tent alone. The Anthony Nolan Trust ran a donor recruitment clinic on site to raise awareness of leukaemia as one of the biggest causes of death in children in the UK. The Anthony Nolan Trust is committed to increasing the number of Asians on their donor register, therefore Bradford Mela was an ideal event to reach out to the South Asian communities. The zones doubled up as creative spaces offering visual arts, photography and gaming activities for children – giving parents thinking space to connect with local organisations.

**Family enjoying kulfi ice-cream** | Bradford Mela | 2005 | © Tim Smith

**Hafia! were an ensemble of 50 outstanding musicians, dancers, acrobats and craftspeople who celebrated Morocco's rich blend of Arab, Berber and African traditions** | Bradford Mela | 1994 | © Tim Smith

**Members of The Caste Folk Musicians of Rajasthan performing traditional folk songs in Lister Park**
Bradford Mela | 1997 | © Tim Smith

## Nurturing Local Talent

Bradford and Nottingham Melas have prioritised showcasing local talent from the beginning. Around 62% of artists performing at the 2009 Bradford Mela were local, and the number is increasing year by year. Katherine Canoville is a part of Bradford Mela's programming team and is committed to combining major artists with home grown talent. She says this is not only an excellent opportunity to showcase local talent, but also makes good financial sense. *"I think the emphasis to bring our local artists up through the Mela channel is absolutely crucial to the longevity of the Mela. We're working on smaller budgets for a much larger event, so it's crucial that we nurture our local artists. It's not a case of, 'Let's use them because they're second best'. It's a case of, 'We've got exactly the quality we need already, let's put things around it, as opposed to get the big international artists and then chuck a few local artists in. It's the reverse thinking. Build our Mela around our local artists and then get our guests."*

**Nottingham Asian Arts Council young dhol troupe** | Nottingham Mela | 2004 | © Alan Lodge

Ajay Chhabra is Artistic Director of nutkhut and London Mela. He reveals that some mela organisers more than others, feel a particular sense of responsibility to offer a platform to local talent: *"I get phone calls regularly from young people saying, 'Can you put our work on?' If I don't book those young people, where are they going to go? Twenty or so years ago, I was one of those young people picking up the phone and asking, 'Can I perform at your event?' So it's really really important that I always keep that at the back of my mind – and the least I can do is respond and follow things through. What you see now at the London Mela is that those I booked for the Community Stage in 2003 when they were ten or eleven are now seventeen or eighteen and performing on the Radio 1 Stage or the Main Stage or the Classical Music Stage. They've kind of progressed onto the more professional stages, and that is very satisfying."*

Melas play a leading role in boosting local creativity by nurturing local talent. They have the potential to build entire cultural industries around them, as was reflected by the emergence of street arts, when Bradford Festival first began with all its component events in 1987. The Festival offered a platform to street artists as well as an opportunity for employment in the creative industries. For example, mela plays a vital role in developing local talents, like Skinning the Cat and Nachda Punjab, as professional performers. However, the closure of the Bradford Festival brought with it an enormous loss, as Ben Pugh, Producer of the Bradford Mela explains: *"It's the same in every city – you close down theatres, you take away festivals, you stop doing the parade and what you find very quickly is*

*those in the creative industries - the carnival makers, the street theatre performers, the musicians, the sound engineers, whatever it is – very often live hand to mouth anyway. They lose an opportunity to do a job in the city. The Mela's a showcase of not just the city's creativity, but it also inspires those creative practitioners by bringing excellent stuff from around the world to complement that. That needs to be fed by a community that is conscious of, and committed to, and involved in developing the Mela. It's become even more important in the last three or four years, because Bradford has a fairly sparse creative calendar. It's the only really big opportunity for the whole of the district's arts and cultural sector to show what they're made of, to have a chance to contribute, and to be seen in public by a lot of people. It's the big opportunity to get in front of audiences."*

**Local talent at the Nottingham Mela** | 2004 | © Alan Lodge

**A masked dancer from the Channi-Upuli Dance Ensemble performing a Sri Lankan folk tale**
Bradford Mela | 1998 | © Tim Smith

## Designing the Mela

The design of the majority of melas in Britain is
perfunctory – little thought is given to the site
layout beyond determining where the mela
infrastructure – stages, stalls, barriers, portaloos -
needs to be set up. For a small minority of melas, it
is the attention given to their design which sets
them apart. Bradford Mela in particular has a
design legacy from its relationship with the
Bradford Festival. Over the years, the Mela's site
design in particular has attracted delegations from
as far afield as Edinburgh and Nottingham.

Bradford Mela Producer, Ben Pugh, believes that the key to designing a mela is to offer a holistic experience to the audience: *"This is the art of programming mela rather than the specific detail of programming a stage at a mela. All the elements have to work together. Making it look, sound and feel creatively and artistically right is the key driver. The feeling that being on site gives you is as much part of the experience of the event as who's performing on stage or what food you eat. It's the ambiance that is created by making sure that things are laid down in the right way, that there's not too big a gap from here to there, or that there's no great spaces of undefined openness. When they arrive on site, what's the first thing they see? What's the noise they hear? What's the smell they get? Where are the colours? What's drawing their attention? What's pulling them through the event? So as an audience member, they're able to easily and comfortably relax into an environment which feels probably smaller than the event actually is. So it's about a flow of people through an engaging and captivating space."*

Two of the earliest Directors of Bradford Festival, Dusty Rhodes and Allan Brack, wanted to use their background in theatre to make the Bradford Festival Finale and Mela a sensory experience. They devised innovative ways of "dressing" the Victorian park with sculptural pieces and decorative gateways to create a "visual feast". In doing so, the team also introduced colourful visual arts to the events. Dusty Rhodes explains: *"The visual impact is really important. We're dressing the park. We're putting the tigers on the gates. We've got Lulu the Indian Elephant. What do you expect when you're bringing people into a party?*

*You expect balloons, you expect decor of some sort, streamers and things if you're talking about somebody's house. But if you're talking about a park, you want a visual feast. It wants to look festive. It needs to look like it never looks at other times of the year. It wants to look visually exciting. We want to lift people's spirits. We want them to feel that there's a special moment going on. We wanted to create a sense of colour and atmosphere. We had decorative gateways to create a definite entrance, to mark the actual space. Archways are ceremonial; they usher people down paths. Because it was dark we could put festoon lighting between the arches and through the trees, and create a sort of walkway. It gave the whole thing a sort of physical presence."*

Dusty Rhodes' experience of building structures and stages for the Festival and Mela culminated in building the iconic Stage on the Lake in Lister Park. This provided the focus of the Festival Finale – an annual theatrical extravaganza featuring a firework display. Dusty Rhodes' hands-on approach is evident here as he explains how the structure was created: *"We liked the idea of the lake. There was a natural amphitheatre that ran down to it, and it also looked like a good setting for that sort of finale extravaganza large scale multimedia show. There's a particular moment if it's a calm evening, where there's a stillness that descends over the lake and it gives up some of its heat and there's a slight steam that hangs in the air. And sound travels beautifully because it's slightly dampened – the echo goes out of the air, if you like. And it's wonderful to use that moment of calm to do things in, because you can really use it theatrically. You can go from diminuendos to great crescendos both in terms of light and sound. So we could see the opportunities for that. When we first said this is what we want to do, somebody from the council said we couldn't do that because we'd puncture the puddling clay and cause flooding! I had to get dressed up in my wet suit and take some samples of the clay from the bottom of the lake up to the university, so they could do a load of stress testing on it. And we worked it out basically. So we built a structure on the lake and put a platform on it. Then what we would do is bring a load of barrels on to that platform, pump water from the lake into those barrels, so we would replicate the loading that would go onto it when the rest of the structure was built. Then we would allow the whole thing to sink for about a week. And then we would tip all the barrels over, go back underneath, readjust all the levels to make it level, and then build the rest of the stage. I really don't know where we got the energy from, because we were also going in and converting the Wool Exchange and decorating that, and putting up archways in the city centre and doing the rest of the park!"*

**Enjoying a fairground ride** | Bradford Mela | 1988 | © Tim Smith

**Aerial trapeze act Skinning the Cat** | Bradford Mela | 1991 | © Tim Smith

**A mobile sculpture moving through the crowds in Gunnersbury Park** | London Mela | 2005 | © Tim Smith

**Site breakdown** | Nottingham Mela | 1993 | © Nadeem Haider/APNA Arts

**Members of the British Raj aboard their camel entertain crowds** | Bradford Mela | 2001 | © Tim Smith

## Spacescapes

Bradford Mela incorporates sixteen hours of programming across multiple locations over the two day event. The Mela is keen to build better relationships with its diverse audiences, therefore it now gives detailed thought to the individual needs of its audience segments - children, families, youth, elderly, women. For instance, there must be something on offer for each family member from around midday to 9pm. Neither is the Mela demographic a constant – the flow of people changes throughout the day, and the programming needs to reflect this. Planning and programming a mela of this scale and diversity is very different to programming, for instance, a one stage youth music event.

Bradford Mela now adopts a structured yet highly sophisticated approach to creating stylised spaces that will simultaneously cater for different audience groups. Offering a balanced artistic programme is vital for attracting diverse audiences and keeping them there. Creating unique 'spaces' to complement specific mela elements or genres can deepen audience engagement and help create more fulfilling experiences. Bradford Mela's Music Programmer, Katherine Canoville, says the organisers really want the public to access as much of the Mela as possible, by trying out the different spaces: *"The whole arena is now the main stage and we plan it with a view that everybody can sample everything. We don't want anyone to feel they're playing on a secondary stage, we really don't. We want all the stages to be valid."*

Markets are a crucial part of the mela experience and traders know all too well that melas offer the public the right ambience to browse and shop. Bradford Mela's market is currently the largest market event in Bradford's annual calendar. Around 100 traders were booked for the 2009 Mela and the event often attracts European traders selling the usual fare of jewellery, clothing, unstitched fabric, handicrafts, footwear and religious goods. Known as 'mela travellers', about a quarter of the traders at Bradford Mela have stalls at every mela on the 'circuit', setting up at a different mela every weekend throughout the summer mela season. Food stalls account for just over a quarter of all stalls. While it is common for food stalls to be scattered around the entire mela site, all food traders at Bradford Mela are now kept together, in a similar way to a food court, offering everything from burgers and chips to curries that showcase

regional specialities of the Indian subcontinent. The Mela organisers say that keeping all the food stalls together also makes life easier for litter pickers since all refuse is in one location.

Arts development agency Kala Sangam, is one of the Bradford Mela partners. It takes over an intimate marquee, running taster sessions in a variety of artforms. Kala Sangam sees its role as making the Mela experience informal by offering the public a chance to sample something new, and thereby making the Mela experience more interactive. Ajit Singh from Kala Sangam explains: *"Getting people to work with an artist on a one-to-one level rarely happens at melas - you just see them on stage. We're the interface between the artist and the audience, so we introduce the audiences to artforms, and we get them working with artists who you traditionally wouldn't be able to get close to. So they get to see a performance and have a hands-on activity."*

Keranjeet Kaur Virdee of South Asian Arts UK programmed classical fusion band Indus at the 2009 Bradford Mela on the Classical Stage (also known as the Sunset Stage). She explains that classical musicians need a certain ambience to have a creative impact. The Classical Stage was set within a bohemian style tent in order to create a 'mehfil', an intimate space with a code of conduct traditional in the Mughal Courts: *"A mehfil is a bit like if you had somebody come to your lounge and do a small live music performance, and everyone's sitting around cross legged on the floor, sharing a cup of tea and just indulging in the music. It's a very Victorian chamber music type of feeling. The artist is at close proximity in front of you, on a*

**Preparing masala dosas at an Indian food stall** | Bradford Mela | 1994 | © Tim Smith

low stage, where you can actually have that direct conversation. The audience is made to feel valued. There may be two people sitting out there at first and it ends up with fifteen or sixteen in a crowd afterwards, but there is that conversation, and the audience feel that they're sharing that space with the artist."

Najma Akhtar explains that she performs better knowing the audience can enjoy a particular style of music in the way it's meant to be appreciated: *"It's the traditional aspect of sitting down with bolster cushions. They're relaxed and they want to hear you in a comfortable setting that's appropriate to the intimate sound. It brings the audience to me and I like a little bit of closeness. There's more of a connection. There isn't that distance and I think it's to do with spirituality and it's to do with calmness and it's to do with listening and it's to do with quality and clarity of the music. There's more control on the sound quality if you have a limited space. If melas have that in place then I can easily go and do a set even without my band, but just as a semi classical ghazal traditional thing."*

The street arts central to the original Bradford Festival remain a fundamental part of the Bradford Mela. Ben Pugh explains that he thinks of street arts as part and parcel of the Mela design, and plants performances around the site to bring the environment to life: *"From the moment they walk in to the gate the audience should feel like they're being transported into a different world. They're at a festival, in a celebratory environment. Street theatre or outdoor art is designed and performed specifically for an outdoor environment. It might be theatre, dance, parade or carnival or performance*

*work. So the advantage of that is you can animate the environment the audience are walking around in. It's something that should be around every corner to engage people, and that to me is what makes something a festival, something that is more than just a stage and a bunch of stalls. So when they go from the Mango Stage, they walk through the avenue of stalls towards the Sunrise Stage. And along the way, they pass a samba band playing and they see over in the corner a guy doing a plate balancing act. People make their own performance arena so they go out and they define where they're going to do their show, and we bring in artists who are experts in that field. So we have at one extreme the people that come and put up their suitcase and do their juggling show, and at the other extreme we have people like the Rajasthani Circus Troupe that we had on site in 2009, who mark out a big pitch, and they do some great Rajasthani style balancing on a tall pole and walking across tightrope - you know proper circus stuff in the open air! Originally street theatre was very much about taking it out of the theatre and putting it out on the street, and engaging with the audience in a different way. It comes back to that relationship again between audience and performer, and for us, taking it off the stage and putting it on the grass, putting it amongst the people, is very much about creating a festival. It's about creating an atmosphere out of a constant source of interests and entertainment."*

The 2009 Bradford Mela included Movieplex, a piece of live art set inside two shipping containers, which was symbolic of taking indoor work outdoors. One of the containers was a high-tech museum which led into a plush 1920s art deco style Victorian musical cinema, complete with a screen and authentic pull-down seating for eighteen people. Although Ajay Chhabra did not create the work especially for Bradford Mela, he felt the novelty of the work made it perfect for the environment. The work encapsulated the sorts of unusual and sometimes unexpected experiences and spaces a mela can offer to its audience.

*"People don't quite expect to see two big fat shipping containers in a park. It takes people out of their daily lives, out of what they know and constantly draw on. Because a festival is ephemeral - it exists only for that period of time - it can become unfamiliar even to the trained eye so you really can put stuff on there that people wouldn't otherwise expect. It's provocative. If people come to a mela leaving behind all the stresses and strains of the past week of work or family or whatever, for those few hours they can just be transported to somewhere else. They see an artist live on stage that they listen to in the car all the time. They eat some food that they really are fond of, being cooked in front of them, fresh. They bump into an old school friend or a family member. They walk into a shipping container and they see this show that they may not otherwise come across.*

*They queue up and they saw it, and then they went home and discovered a further digital experience about the show online. A completely alternative experience! You couldn't even make that up, could you!"*

# Developing new work

World music activist Katherine Canoville regards mela as an ideal space to explore fusion. She describes fusion as, *"putting together the traditional with the contemporary in order to make it more appealing to the masses and particularly to young people."* This marriage between the unfamiliar and the familiar creates a brilliant opportunity for collaboration and cultural understanding, and Katherine feels this is precisely the ethos of mela. *"By putting contemporary artists that draw people in around some key traditional artists, it allows us to raise the platform of the artists who are playing their traditional music for people who might not normally go to see them. When they hear the modern day version of a track they remember their grandparents listening to, they'll embark on their own musical journey to find out a little bit more about where that singer came from and embrace other types of music. Many musicians who are culturally diverse are embracing each other's traditional music, and this is where the fusion - the melting pot if you like - is created. They throw these sounds into a kind of a sound sphere, and come up with something that bounces back which is basically what fusion is."*

**Akademi Dance performance** | Nottingham Mela | 2009 | © Jagdish Patel/Frontline Images

Radio One DJ, Bobby Friction first visited Nottingham Mela as a contemporary art student at Nottingham Trent University. He returned to Nottingham Mela in 2005 with Classical Friction, a fusion of live classical music by The East Midlands Orchestra ViVA with his own Asian underground beats. Bobby savoured the opportunity of collaborating in this way. *"I remember just going, 'Wow, I've got a blank canvas! Unique space! This is brilliant!' As someone who comes from the club side of the arts spectrum, until then I was still used to having people go, 'You're a contractor, you've come to my club, here's the money, I kind of want you to do this!' This was the first time I've had, 'We've got a mela coming up, let's create something interesting, what do you think?'"*

One of the greatest challenges for Bobby Friction was to ensure the performance that emerged from this unique collaboration did not alienate the Mela audience. *"It was totally inspirational. The audience were mixed Asian and white people, and I thought a lot of the young street kids, the funky kids would go, 'This is an absolute load of bullshit. It has nothing to do with me!' But they absolutely loved it. The sense of spectacle for the audience, more than anything else, was seeing an orchestra in the middle of their city centre, a full twenty-six piece orchestra, all dressed up! Most people haven't seen an orchestra. I hadn't seen a full orchestra until I actually met up with ViVA. For me, it was definitely the dancers and the orchestra and just the iconography of people going, 'OK, there's an orchestra there but that guy is actually playing decks so this is something that I can relate to'. And it kind of taught me that if you can put on a big enough spectacle and take your art seriously,*

*you can broadcast your art to anyone in your community, not just people who think like you!"*

Indy Hunjan runs Kala Phool, an arts development agency, which has carried out a lot of strategic development with the national mela sector. She says that developing new work, particularly in the mela context, can have a profound effect on the artist as well as the audience. *"When you're talking about commissions it's a much deeper experience with the mela, it's a much deeper experience within the community that the mela sits within. Because the artists that have been brought together are being asked to consider the environment that they're going to be producing in, delivering in, they have to understand their audience. It's very much a shared process between the mela and the artist although the artists have the autonomy to do their thing, that's why they're being brought on board."*

When Alan Tweedie was Artistic Director of Edinburgh Mela, he was committed to creating new work which, he says, is vital to keeping melas fresh and relevant. *"Melas will be stale if we see the same things every year. You need the infusion of time, of new ideas and of new happenings."*

Tony Lidington programmes street arts into the Bradford Mela. He believes the mela offer rests on its artistic merit, so it is imperative for mela to continue to reinvent itself. *"If it doesn't keep offering new things, then it'll become less attractive and people will simply not bother because they're coming to the same thing year on year. And if you've been to it one year, you don't need to go to it the next. And it has to be something that people are attracted to from afar* because there's no point coming to an event in Bradford if you could see it in Birmingham or Manchester or Berlin or Norway."

Developing new work is also important for artists, as Skinder Hundal explains: *"At the New Art Exchange, we are very interested in creating new ways of working, advancing the artform, exploring subject matter. We look at gender, inter-religious or religious conflict, untold stories of marginalised communities. The artforms that we present are predominantly visual but connect with the performing arts as well. We are challenging and stretching the artists, so the artist's reputation is growing. So the mela could be a really really powerful vehicle because it's got established audiences......mela has developed a role for itself to challenge the developing Asian communities. It's the point at which you've got a main audience and a niche audience coming together and connecting."*

It is precisely for these challenges that collaborating in a mela setting is attractive to singer Najma Akhtar: *"When you collaborate with another artist from a different genre, you are immediately exposing yourself to that person's genre. Like let's say I did something with Basement Jaxx, it would immediately connect me to them and their audience. There is a crossover of ideas and sounds and you immediately get a different kind of a take on a song. If I sing a ghazal song with a tabla and harmonium and then I do it with my band, it's a different thing than doing it with a rap artist or an R&B arranger or with an orchestra. Immediately the whole dynamic of the song changes and that challenges me as an artist. It's all very easy for me to sing an Indian song and put a drum and bass loop under it. Bu=t the challenging thing to do is to take a different genre and to try and manipulate my voice around that melody."*

As Najma Akhtar and Bobby Friction reveal, collaborations can offer many possibilities from the artist's perspective - an exchange of technique, the experience of a different artform, the chance to challenge their practice; or a chance to rethink their offer before presenting it to a new audience. Developing new work like this is also critical for mela organisations themselves. Melas depend on exchanges and collaborations – locally, nationally and internationally - to increase their knowledge and expertise. Focussing on networking and partnership furthers their programming skills and range. It is also important to make connections with the mela's South Asian roots – but new and interesting connections which reach beyond merely programming an artist into an empty slot.

For instance, when Alan Tweedie was Artistic Director of Edinburgh Mela, he connected a Chinese musician from the city's university with a Pashtun violinist and a sitar player from Pakistan. Alan linked them with a Scottish musician, as musical director, with whom he had worked on an earlier project. Initially, the musicians discussed and exchanged folk tunes by post and email. The task for the musicians was to fuse the final piece with their own traditions. They met in Edinburgh for ten days leading up to the Mela, where they fused the music further across the three traditions, to create a fifty minute piece called Sounds in Many Lands. *"When it came out as a concert, you really couldn't tell what was Chinese, Scottish or Pashtun. It was seamless."* Crucially, the process of identifying artists, and then building and sustaining relationships with them requires long term activity, which in turn requires investment.

As mela is made up of different artforms rather than being an artform itself, it has historically struggled to attract core funding. Without support for infrastructure, mela organisations lead a hand to mouth existence and have to find innovative approaches year on year to survive, which damages their ability to create exciting collaborations and commissions. Furthermore, with their coming of age, melas recognise the need for long term strategies. However, melas cannot afford the thinking time. Having a long-term funding commitment would enable melas to be more strategic in their planning, be more cost effective, and have a long term vision, instead of existing hand to mouth. This dilemma is further exacerbated by delayed local authority budget announcements, which can cut into planning and development time for melas. Sheena Wrigley, previously Head of Theatres, Arts and Festivals for Bradford Council, knows this scenario only too well. *"We were often waiting till February or March to know what budgets we were working with and therefore what we could commit to the Mela. It's a fact of life in local authority but it makes it very difficult when you're trying to develop a mela, especially when you're trying to create new work or commission artists."* It is difficult for melas to develop exciting and high quality projects in this sort of environment.

Partly in response to this, the European Mela Network was established to advocate for melas and promote collaborative working. The network – with Bradford, Nottingham and London at the forefront – offers an opportunity for dialogue rather than the chance to generate product. For instance in 2009, Nottingham Glasgow and Bradford Melas programmed their events on three consecutive weekends and jointly funded a Gujarati folk troupe on a three week visit – something they would have struggled to afford otherwise. The troupe spent a week in each city, running workshops in schools and community centres.

**Classical Friction** | Bobby Friction with the Viva Orchestra | Nottingham Mela | 2005 | © ArtReach

## Social Conscience

A sense of social responsibility pervades some contemporary melas, which are organically engaging with wider political debates. It is apt that constructive dialogue about sustainability should occur at a point where community comes together, not least because melas are subsidised through public money. Ajay Chhabra is Artistic Director of London Mela and founder chair of the European Mela Network. He believes mela can play a key role in getting people to reflect on current global issues on a practical level: "If art can do anything, art can make people look at how they live their lives. There are many ways of demonstrating that the mela is sitting around at that political table and it isn't just a small community event."

Belfast Mela adopts an underlying green theme to each year's event, and has for example, worked with local partners to raise awareness of recycling and local produce. The 2009 London Mela used solar power to run one of its generators, and is currently researching alternatives to diesel fuel. London Mela has also been working with local authorities over a number of years on a major campaign to encourage visitors to use public transport to visit the event. Meanwhile, Bradford Mela purchases all its bottled water from FRANK, a pioneering social enterprise that donates 100% of its profits to providing clean water in India.

Politics has always been at the heart of Nottingham Mela. Apna Arts organised a young person's festival called True Azadi in 1999, instead of a mela, to heighten awareness of issues of equality. The event was held on 14th and 15th August which tied in with Independence Day celebrations in India and Pakistan. The publicity literature used the slogan *"Azadi (Freedom) is the theme, staying TRUE (Tolerance, Respect, Unity and Equality) is the message"*.

Bradford Mela linked up Christian Aid and Islamic Relief charities in 2006 so they could campaign jointly. Bradford Mela Producer Ben Pugh believes this collaboration helped to build bridges organically. *"They were both campaigning against the same thing, at the same time - climate change and drop the debt. By partnering them up, they exhibited together, they campaigned together. The impact of that was phenomenal in terms of broadening people's understanding about the event and what it meant in terms of cohesion. And there were some other tangible things like*

*Christian Aid writing in their national magazine about what a great time they'd had at Bradford Mela. You've got three quarters of a million people that would never even think about coming to Bradford Mela, reading about the organisation they support having a wonderful time there, campaigning alongside Islamic Relief."*

Bradford and Edinburgh Melas have recently started to commission bespoke spaces to engage and entertain families with young children in a meaningful way. In Bradford, this is part of the drive to promote Bradford Mela as a family friendly environment. Alan Tweedie, past Artistic Director of Edinburgh Mela, explains why: *"I think a lot of people feel that children get short changed at mela, that there's not very much that actually connects creatively with children, and quite often it's done in an under resourced way. There's no effort to create that special magic moment for the child."* The 2009 Bradford Mela showcased The Hive, a zone that was themed around bees and pollination, which also incorporated important social messages. This was an area for young families to explore together - adults could only enter the zone if accompanied by children. A range of arts-based activities took children on a journey through the life of a bee. Children were invited to dress up in a beekeeper's outfit and to talk to a real beekeeper; they could use seeds to make rangoli style butterflies, bees and flowers on the floor; they could plant seeds to take home; or they could make a kazoo out of junk and participate in a performance with a buzz band within the zone. Tony Lidington is part of Bradford Mela's programming team, and was responsible for bringing The Hive to the Bradford Mela.

He explains that the subtle social messaging helped to enhance The Hive's educational potential. *"It wasn't, 'You've got to learn about global warming!' It was: 'Here are a range of activities that happen to be linked to the fact that there's a problem with bees dying. And it's useful for people to know about pollination and bee dances and stuff.' So it was a hook on which to hang a vision. The messaging is simply something to hang it around and is visually interesting and artistically easy to connect with. The context in which things are placed is what gives it political meaning."*

# Arts of the the Mela

## Performance and Dance

Dance has always been an important component of mela. From the outset, traditional bhangra folk dance groups have been popular. One such troupe, Nachda Punjab, have regularly performed at Bradford and many other melas. Some twenty-five years ago, when they decided to form, they approached Oriental Arts for advice. Champak Kumar encouraged them to find a rehearsal space and work on their choreography, and booked them to perform as soon as they were ready. Nachda Punjab had drawn inspiration from 'authentic' dance troupes in the Punjab, such as Mela Punjab Da – a twenty-two strong troupe of colourfully dressed male and female street artists and stage performers offering a combination of folk song and dance. As the word 'mela' in their title signifies, they were formed specifically to perform at melas in India. Champak was delighted to learn that the troupe was already touring in Britain when he was looking for acts to perform at the first Bradford Mela in 1988. It was a unique opportunity to book an internationally acclaimed dance and music troupe to perform at the first Bradford Mela, and set a standard for Oriental Arts to build links with renowned international artists for future melas.

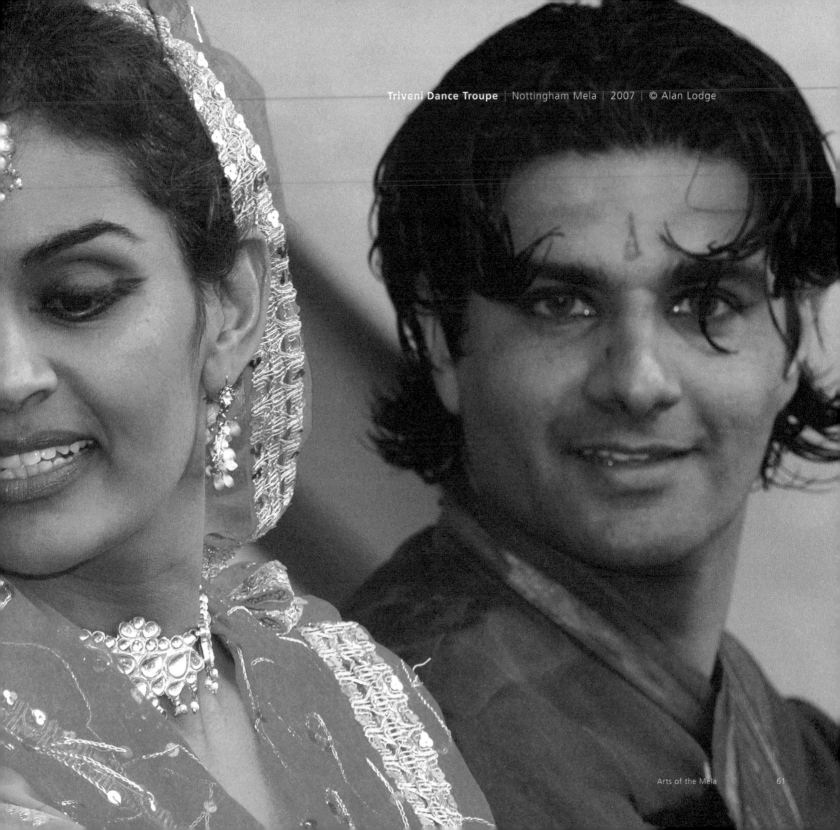

In recent years, Bollywood dance groups have also become popular, not least because of the genre's widening appeal and accessibility which has placed Indian films firmly in the mainstream market. Ironically, it was Bollywood films of the seventies and eighties – which tended to feature a celebratory scene against the backdrop of a mela - that inspired Champak Kumar of Oriental Arts to think about the mela as the ultimate event to encapsulate the vibrancy of Bradford's South Asian communities. Bollywood expert, Professor Rachel Dwyer, considers Bollywood's fascination with mela: *"You know in American films you get the prom being the big thing, and in the older Hindi (Bollywood) films the mela was the big thing. It would be a village fair rather than something in a city – a mixture between a fairground and a market and it would be a really big deal for the village people. It was one of the few times where women got to go out somewhere. They could go to the temple or they could go to get water and there weren't many other things to do. The mela was somewhere girls always went to buy their bangles. There was a chance that you'd meet your beloved there although your dad would only let you go with your girlfriends! And obviously it was still in public but it was the idea of an encounter, and dressing up to go out and be seen, and then the fairground atmosphere. There's all those films called Mela, like the old one with Dilip Kumar and Nargis, and those songs saying, 'Life is like a mela, we come and go'. And there's a song from Khoon Pasina, where Amitabh goes to a mela with Rekha in a sort of village outfit, dressed up to the nines, with lots and lots of people standing around watching them. The mela setting allowed them to meet in a way that they couldn't normally meet but it also allowed them to be looked at by everybody else - you had a spectacle."*

Bradford Mela Producer, Ben Pugh, believes that just like bhangra, Bollywood dancing is well suited to the mela context: *"Very rarely will there be the right environment at a mela for detailed or intimate dance performance to really shine. The mela's an environment where there is noise and bustle and distraction and a very short attention span for audiences. So dance generally has to be a bit showy, a bit open air, a bit kind of in line with the noisy bustle of it. So actually, on our Sunrise Stage, we had Spice Entertainment who are great value in the sense that they do loud, brash, Bollywood hip hop, kind of crossover fusion. They're street dance but Bollywood style. And they're brilliant because they keep the audience engaged and they're young and hip and beautiful. And they're really slick at what they do. That works!"*

Named after a trapeze move, Skinning the Cat are a Bradford based, women only, acrobatic theatre trapeze troupe. Fresh out of art college in Bradford, Becky Truman formed the troupe in 1988 when Bradford Festival Director, Allan Brack, offered her an opportunity to perform at the Festival and Mela. *"Our show wasn't flying trapeze as people might expect in a circus. We used to weave a little mythological story – a very simple storyline - there weren't any words. There was music and it was more like dancing in the air, very theatrical. We'd set up our trapeze rig, this big metal structure, in the park. We would move between different bits of equipment, there would be a lot of spinning and acrobatics and fire and lights and some effects like smoke or whatever. The rig was quite decorative,* very gaudy bright colours with bits of mirrors stuck on it so it caught the light and it was embellished with creatures and colours and all sorts. We had costumes which portrayed characters within the story, often animalistic. I used to buy a lot of fabric to make the costumes from the Asian shops to fit in with the look of the mela. The night time shows were the best because everything sparkled."

Mela can be a demanding environment in which to make dance work, particularly for classical forms, however they have still played an important role in the mela story. Balbir Singh, a kathak trained dancer and choreographer, has regularly worked with Bradford Mela. He explains that in order to make the work accessible, a dancer has to bring a different set of skills to performing outdoors than would be required in a theatre space: *"If you're making work in theatre, it's very much playing with the hidden as well as the visible. It's very much three dimensional. Even if it's a big theatre there's a sense of intimacy and pulling the energy and focus inwards, and lighting design is very much part of that, you know that black box setting. If you don't necessarily perform or project well, you can get away with that in a theatre space - if they're really engaged in the movement and the material, that in itself is really engaging for your audience to pull them in. But when you're doing work that's on a big scale outdoors, the performance quality a dancer needs to have is very different from performing in a theatre. There's less depth and dimension and you have to project the energy a lot more so the audience can read it. It's great being a fantastic dancer but if you can't pull the audience's eye towards you then you get lost in the space. Although you can have moments of*

intimate smaller scale movement, the main focus is the whole body and also covering a big space as a group of dancers, so you don't become invisible. Then you have the aesthetic of pacing it to keep the audience interested. It should be alright for the audience to dip in and out of the material in terms of coming half way through without it losing a sense of experience for them. It's giving them some kind of hook."

Mela organisers deliberately try to work with artists that are renowned for pushing the boundaries. Pratap Pawar is internationally recognised for his fusion of kathak with flamenco dance and has just been awarded the Padma Shri, India's most prestigious award. Although he has performed at Nottingham Mela several times, he recalls one episode in particular: *"The last time I was at Nottingham a downpour threatened our show and there was only a handful of people in the audience. With the Grace of God it stopped raining at exactly quarter to three. Come four o'clock the Mayor was seated and there must have been about 1,500 people in the audience. A show at the mela has to be louder, visually more colourful, so I keep the tabla and I also bring in an African drummer, an Afro-Caribbean drummer, a South Indian drummer. So on that rainy day in Nottingham I thought, 'My footwork alone won't be enough to mesmerise this crowd; they need something more to pull them in.' I said, 'The rain may have stopped but still I want to show you rain!' I did my footwork. I had two mics on my ghungroo (ankle bells), so the audience could hear my footwork in time with the rhythm of four drummers. And with hand gestures I created a cloud, a flash of thunder, and then a downpour of rain! The audience was with me then."*

Akademi is a pioneering dance company producing innovative large-scale, site specific shows, perfect for the mela environment. Their recent show, Initium, was performed in high streets and shopping centres as well as melas including London and Nottingham. This contemporary spectacle featured a cast of dancers and was made to adapt to, and transform, each space it encountered. The Artistic Director, Mira Kaushik, explains that the show was a steep learning curve for the company: *"It is the most liberating activity that Akademi has done. It's a very very flexible group of dancers. Every time you go to a new site the show becomes a new experience. So now we've got that experience of adjusting to the site, and that's a major intention and focus of our operation as well - that if we are performing we are part of the local backdrop really."* The success of Initium has enthused Mira to consider the possibility of creating work specifically for melas. *"Because we are not selling ticketed shows, melas are an appropriate site for us to take our work to and reach out to a larger group of people. I am now hoping that I manage to put ten melas together to collectively commission something which then we can go and perform in every mela. It's going to be new, it's going to be cost effective, and it is something which has got their commissioning ownership. For us, it is taking our work to a whole new world of people where we try and reach out."*

**Nahid Siddique** | Nottingham Mela | 1992 | © Nadeem Haider/APNA Arts

**Kala Chethena Kathakali Dance Troupe** | Nottingham Mela | 1992 | © Nadeem Haider/APNA Arts

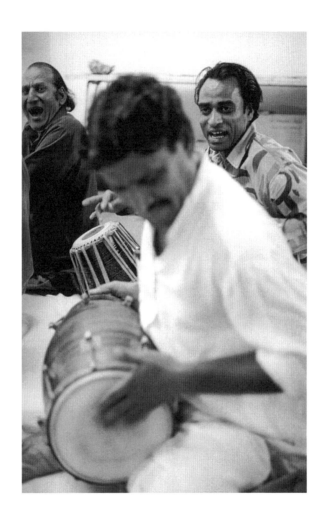

**Apna Arts Touring Project** | Nottingham Mela | 1994 | © Nadeem Haider/APNA Arts

# Visual Arts

As well as being a member of Nottingham Mela's programming team, David Thomas is Senior Curator of the New Art Exchange. It is therefore not surprising that he was keen to introduce innovative contemporary art to the Mela audience: *"We feel mela is a perfect opportunity to introduce cutting edge work to Asian audiences. I'm not saying they're coming for that. We have to make sure that the core part of the family oriented mela is there because they're coming to see Malkit Singh. But they'll bump into something else and it's introducing them. So we're not expecting these huge audiences to come and see the more experimental pieces but we would like that even five percent of the audience who see them would go back and say, 'Wow! That was amazing! I'd love to see more of that!'"*

Fabric, Bradford's arts development agency, works in partnership with Bradford Mela to programme visual arts into the Mela. Director Gideon Seymour talks about some of the challenges of taking contemporary art into a mela. *"The way visual arts play a part in the Mela is going to have to be on*

**Chila Burman's ice-cream cones (art installation)** | Nottingham Mela | 2007 | © Ashok Mistry

*the Mela's terms. We are not going to create a perfectly lit white box with peace and quiet for people to step back and contemplate large canvases, but why would you want to put an exhibition at the Mela that you could see in a traditional gallery? The Mela is a two day event. Surely the point of that is to do something that's site specific. You don't get that opportunity the rest of the year so I think the point about the Mela is that it gives us the opportunity to do things differently. That's about different ways of showing work, it's about large scale, it's about projection in tents as part of a performance. I think the Mela's got to be about mixtures. It's got to be about where artforms cross over and come together. It's got to be about energy and excitement and new experiences, and making use of the setting rather than trying to make the setting work with our traditional visions of how art should be appreciated. For those people that are willing to take up the challenge it's an interesting way of working."*

In 2005, Fabric worked with Bradford Festival (of which the Mela was then a part) to create the Bradford Arts Trail. The aim was to showcase local artistic talents by inviting artists to open up their homes, studios and galleries to members of the public for the ten day festival. A centrally located art gallery was also available for artists without space, where they could showcase and sell their work. Not only was this an original way of taking the festival into the community, it also provided an opportunity for artists to connect with their community. Around sixty artists participated in the scheme in artforms ranging from textiles, jewellery, sculpture, printmaking to multimedia.

David Thomas's ambitious plans to reinvigorate Nottingham Mela's visual arts programme involved a marquee, adapted to offer gallery standard exhibition space as well as an area for family workshops. The space was used in 2007 to show Chila Burman's ice-cream themed prints, artworks, video installation and a specially commissioned sculptural piece featuring glitter cones. As an extension to the exhibition, her multimedia ice-cream van was 'parked' outside the marquee. Chila acted as guide and encouraged people to interact with the installation: *"You know how you have ice-cream vans at melas? Well, I thought it would be interesting to have an art installation which was an ice-cream van and it sits amongst all the other ice-cream vans. And it's quite interesting the way people came up to it expecting to buy an ice-cream! Then I told them it was a work of art. Two or three people can stand in there so I was going, 'Open the door and go inside!' People were really nosey! You do get lots of Asians because they're looking at it and they can spot an Indian feel to it and they're all going, 'What is this?' They were asking me all about my family and my dad, you know. How come he had an ice-cream van? And they'd never seen an ice-cream van that connected to Indian stuff! It was like an opportunity to present an ice-cream van in a different way, and I did think it worked better at the mela. It's got more of a festival feel to it and therefore it did fit really well. I think, without showing off, my work does lend itself to melas. It's quite colourful and fun, it's to do with all ages, and the mela is to do with ice-cream and celebration and so the ice-cream project would always be a hit at melas."*

**Traditional Rajasthani dance being performed by the Musafir troupe from India** | Bradford Mela | 1999 | © Tim Smith

**Graffiti workshop with artist Mohammed Ali** | Nottingham Mela | 2006 | © Alan Lodge

# Audience Engagement

For artists working in a participatory way, mela offers an attractive proposition to take their work directly to the audience, especially since barriers to access may prevent the audience from engaging with their work in a gallery space. Nottingham and Bradford Melas have a proven track record of challenging audiences with new work, actively encouraging community participation in the arts, as well as making art as accessible as possible. As Mark Fielding, one time Director of Bradford Festival explains, it was because these values were the core tenets of Bradford Festival and Mela, that a strong tradition of street art emerged around the city: *"Bradford was renowned for its street arts festival so street art companies across Europe used to think it was a real feather in their cap if they managed to get to Bradford. At the time there was quite a resurgence of doing things in the street. It was just a way of doing things that were more visually interesting and exciting and that weren't bound by the confines of theatre or indoor space. And it was also about the idea of democratising art really, and taking things to people, or putting things in environments that were more accessible to people. So if you'd do a street arts festival, it's always a combination of things - you'd have some musicians, some jugglers, some performance artists, a bit of visual art like banners, street decorations, pavement artists and stuff – the very essence of street is to make art accessible."*

Motiroti conceived Plain Magic exclusively to tour Melas. The work was shown at True Azadi Youth Festival in Nottingham in 1999, which replaced

Nottingham Mela that year. This was a series of specially customised marquees with Bollywood billboard style paintings by Kifait Husain. Members of the audience chose a favourite section to be photographed against and were given a polaroid as a momento, with motiroti keeping the other copy to create an independent artwork. Artistic Director of motiroti, Ali Zaidi, found it stimulating to be in the mela environment. *"For those artists who are making work in which they're dealing with identities, or those who are complete suckers for making sure their work is experienced by many, the mela becomes a natural space to present work. You get a complete sense of satisfaction. It's exactly the same content that goes into galleries. You're taking it out bang in the middle of people where there is a great prejudice that this is not the right arts audience. Well actually, they may not be the audience who goes into the museums and galleries, but they understand, and they're absolutely interacting with it! And it's a two way street for me because if I were a punter, I would want to see things for free in the open where I don't feel excluded from going, and where you get a whole breadth of audiences from your grandmas to very young people. It becomes a great incentive to actually show the work there."*

Similarly, mela can help overcome barriers to accessing literature. During the mid 1990s, the Yorkshire region's Black Literature Festival was held annually within the main Festival at Lister Park. Anjum Malik was Black Literature Officer at the time, tasked with taking poetry into the community. *"You've got this fabulous Asian community which comes out in huge crowds so you've got this fantastic captive audience who love poetry anyway, and then you've got all the other communities. It's an ideal place for live performance poetry."* Nowadays, Anjum uses the informal atmosphere that melas create, to recruit participants for poetry workshops. *"It's part of the work with the community. That's where the community's going to be so why not go there and stand there and talk to them? I've done that in loads of places. And people will just wander up and talk to you then, won't they! And if they can talk to you they'll think, 'Ok, so if Anjum's running it, she looks like one of us, I think I might attend that workshop and go and see what it's about'."*

The Victoria and Albert Museum have turned to a number of melas as part of their audience development programme. When the museum launched a Sikh exhibition in 1988, featuring some of their most iconic objects significant to Sikhs, it wanted to find a way to reach the Sikh community so they ran a stall at a Sikh Mela in Thetford to publicise the exhibition. However, the V&A wanted to sustain that momentum of widening participation so it negotiated a stall in the Heritage Tent at London Mela. Museum staff ran a series of interactive activities which created the opportunity for dialogue and a lasting relationship. Results of the activity were shown at the museum so participants from the London Mela could be invited back. Eithne Nightingale, Head of Diversity Strategy at the V&A explains: *"There's a theory behind it. It's to show that museums are interactive places, that they are fun, and it's a real engagement. You create something at the Mela, you bring it back into the museum and then people come back to the museum, as opposed to just giving out leaflets and not knowing if they've been thrown away."*

**Children doing traditional block printing** | Bradford Mela | 2004 | © Tim Smith

## Promoting the Arts Industry

Mela doesn't simply act as a showcase; it also helps to promote the industry as a potential profession. One of the core aims of Apna Arts in establishing the Nottingham Mela, was to stimulate employment and training facilities for young people. Given Nottingham and Bradford Melas's strong focus on different artforms, both melas have remained committed to demystifying the notion that art is highbrow, by encouraging engagement and participation at a grassroots level. They are keen to expose young people to the arts, particularly in a community where engagement with arts is traditionally low, and a career in the profession is not taken seriously.

When Ali Zaidi took motiroti's Plain Magic to melas, he realised he was inspiring young people to think beyond the stereotypical South Asian career options. *"There were so many people who brought their parents back into the installation and said, 'Look, these guys are artists and they have been doing this, and they do many other things. Isn't this fantastic?' It's a source of inspiration for the younger generation to go, 'Well actually, if somebody else is making this part of their profession and they're following their passion, and are successful at doing that, why can't we do it?"*

**Lyrikool Lips** | Nottingham Mela | 2009 | © Bartosz Kali

Chila Burman likes to act as a guide, in effect becoming part of her art. She noticed the audience connected with her ice-cream themed work more strongly after realising that the project had been inspired by her Liverpudlian roots. *"People have stereotypes of us. Some people assume that if I've been to art school, I'm a rich girl and my dad's a doctor! One girl thought my dad owned an ice-cream factory. She couldn't get her head around the fact that he had a van and he went on the streets. People would say, 'You're Indian! Your dad was in the ice-cream trade! How did that happen?' So in a way, that was a good reason for having an ice-cream van at a mela, because it turns everything on its head. It disrupted the whole view of what an artist's background is."*

The melas are also committed to inspiring young people to consider careers in arts administration, all part and parcel of running a mela. As a seasoned Apna Arts volunteer, David Thomas understands why melas need to be working with young people: *"Something driven by young people is likely to be new, fresh, stimulating. Their passion is important for the future of melas."* Ben Pugh describes the philosophy at Bradford Mela of involving young people behind the scenes: *"We need to be looking at ways of getting young people engaged in the process now while we're still doing what we're doing. Which is why we have forty or so volunteer event ops who are all in their late teens to early twenties who are all event management students, who are really enthusiastic and committed. And they spend two days running around backstage looking after artists because they want to be the next generation of people doing this. Because of the scale of the event, it needs to*

be dealt with by people who are at a certain stage in their career, but people like Champak and I have a responsibility to be providing the opportunities while we're here, for the younger people to get involved and to build the skills and experience and the contacts to grow into the role."*

Naseem Khan is a policy advisor and a previous Head of Diversity at Arts Council England. She emphasises that as well as gaining programming and administration experience, young people need to be skilled up in strategic planning: *"It's being able to look at things in a wider policy context. If you want to run things successfully, you need to embed the capacity and skills within the sector, and have a vision, and be able to see where to take things further. It's also about seeing where mela fits into the whole spectrum of cultural life within a city and within a society, and that it's not just mela for Asians but actually being able to work out how it's also a sort of calling card for wider society."*

Skinder Hundal goes one step further. He believes the way forward for melas is to encompass a broader range of identities and specialisms: *"The mela will only be sustained if it captures the diversity of the voice. Those voices need to be represented with a common goal, and that goal is to create a more ambitious scene, that maybe has a higher state of consciousness in its delivery in terms of creating more of an enlightened engagement, a meaningful engagement, a legacy for the future and an example to the world. That's what we should be aspiring to."*

**Crowd at the main stage where Rishi Rich Project showcases emerging and established British Asian pop artists**
London Mela | 2004 | © Tim Smith

# Soundscapes

## Bhangra

The dawn of Bradford and Nottingham Melas coincided with the golden age of British bhangra music. Bhangra bands dominated melas for a number of years because they were regarded as the first British Asian pop stars. Nottingham Mela relied on bhangra to generate ticket sales and programmed up to ten of the top bhangra bands to headline Bhangra Heatwave.

Ninder Johal from Achanak remembers performing there. *"Apna Arts did bhangra on Saturday deliberately because they knew most bands would be booked on the Sunday for weddings. The Mela was famous because of its big line up, eight or nine top bhangra bands, sort of the la crème de la crème. Where else could you go to get that? And all the main bands wanted to play in front of a great audience in the sunshine, and at the time it was the only opportunity to do this kind of outdoor event - big infrastructure with a stage where you're in control. At Bradford we played on the Saturday night and after we finished, there were fireworks and we were in the middle of a little island - the Stage on the Lake - and it was the most brilliant experience. It was fantastic."*

Balwinder Safri of Safri Boys | Nottingham Mela | 1991 | © Nadeem Haider/APNA Arts

*"We were doing wedding upon wedding upon wedding where you're open to people saying, 'Can you sing this song or that song?' This wasn't the drudgery of a wedding or a nightclub, or the sometimes chaotic universities. The Mela was something to look forward to. It was about putting on a real performance because you played what you wanted to, in a selected time-slot, in the manner that you wanted to.*

*"The Apna Arts promoter would ring and the first question you'd ask is who else is playing because that would indicate the quality of the festival. We know that if it's a good strong line up there's going to be a lot more people turning up and therefore you get a better chance to play in front of a bigger audience. And because Nottingham was a big line up, we got a chance to see who was on before us and sometimes we hung around to see who came on after us. That was the only opportunity we ever had. What it did was it moved records, it increased exposure of the bands, it increased exposure of the whole genre, absolutely paid off, actually played a pivotal role in the early years."*

Apna Arts founder, Parbinder Singh, wanted to create the Asian equivalent of rock bands performing at football stadiums through Bhangra Heatwave. Certainly, Melas became important events for live bands, as Cultural Commentator Dr Rajinder Dudrah explains. *"Live bands really took these melas seriously. I mean they took the gigs seriously but the melas more so because they were a public platform. Chances were, there were the local British Asian radio stations, and occasionally the local mainstream press as well. So really this was an attempt for them to try and up their game*

but also, in a friendly way get one over on their fellow bands. And sometimes there would be some great collaborations in the live sense, so people would kind of freestyle with each other, you know even though the bands were one after the other, occasionally one dholi player from one band would play with another. And those were rare and special occasions just like I suppose would happen at an open-air festival. These were our mini Glastonbury's, these were our open-air rock concerts, but obviously in a more contained and controlled fashion.*

*"It was only when they started venturing out into live events up and down the country that they realised actually they were pop stars in their own right as British Asians. That's when you had friendly rivalries between the Southall scene and the Midlands scene, the London scene, the scene up north and even rivalry between bands – you know Alaap and Heera. Who outdoes who in terms of performance, dress style and professionalism - all these kinds of things. So I think then the melas were a vehicle and a showcase for these bands to perform at, but they also helped generate this idea of a pop industry, a cultural industry which audiences could tap into."*

'Godfather of Bhangra', Channi Singh from Alaap says the big line-ups were also a rare opportunity to size up the competition. *"The big bands were all at melas so I used to watch every band from backstage to gain experience, to see how other people perform, how they interact with people. Everyone had their own way of performing and interacting, who's doing what dance movements, how they speak, performance skills, when a song*

*finishes, how they talk in between. I have my own
particular style and I didn't want to change that
but you know how even the biggest stars watch
their competition, like a boxer will watch videos of
other fights to see their style. Actors do the same
thing - they don't underestimate anybody."*

The earliest melas really helped bhangra bands to
broaden their audience. Before melas, bhangra
bands performed mainly at universities and Sikh
weddings. Melas presented a chance to play in
front of family audiences as well as diverse
communities. Channi Singh explains that early
melas played a huge role in winning over a new fan
base: *"The greatest advantage of the melas was
that the multicultural people could see you. By that
I mean not only Asians but people who can't even
speak Hindi or Punjabi language who had no idea
what bhangra is. We started getting more bookings
from the melas from people who couldn't see us at
private functions. We got so many more bookings
for weddings after that. The melas really helped to
boost our publicity. That then gave us the chance
to tap into corporate events and then it multiplies,
you know."*

**Nottingham audience dancing to bhangra** | Nottingham Mela | 1991 | © Nadeem Haider/APNA Arts

**Nach da Sansaar** | Nottingham Mela | 1990 | © Nadeem Haider/APNA Arts

# Qawwali

Nottingham and Bradford Melas have hosted some
of the world's greatest qawwali ensembles
including Sabri Brothers, Aziz Mian Qawwal and
Nusrat Fateh Ali Khan. Qawwali is a form of Sufi
devotional music popular in South Asia for its
hypnotic rhythm created by a chorus of hand-
clapping qawwals, which can lead listeners to a
state of religious ecstasy. Qawwali was originally
performed at Sufi shrines in South Asia, although
the form has now gained mainstream popularity.

**Ghulam Farid Sabri** | Nottingham Mela | 1991 | © Nadeem Haider/APNA Arts

It is the work of the late Nusrat Fateh Ali Khan that is credited with bringing international exposure to the genre, popularised by his appearances at WOMAD as well as the release of his records on the Real World label. Apna Arts volunteer, Yasmin Nazir remembers that despite being completely unfamiliar with his music, the volunteers had the foresight and good fortune to book Nusrat Fateh Ali Khan for the very first Nottingham Mela. The legendary qawwal's performance, is still regarded as one of the highlights in Nottingham Mela's twenty-one year history: *"Nusrat Fateh Ali Khan was a suggestion made by my dad. He was into qawwalis and he put some of his stuff on and we were like, 'This is awful!' We were into bhangra and it just didn't appeal to our taste. But when dad said, 'What about Nusrat?', to me that was the first real interest he'd shown in what we were doing. And any young person wants to have that kind of approval from their parents, don't they! And so for my dad to show a bit of interest, we latched on to it and thought, 'Ok, if that will mean that dad will be more supportive, then that's what we'll do.' And we went back to Parbinder and he said, 'You know something, he's a huge international artist and if we could convince Nusrat to come, that would be one of the biggest coups!' And really that's how that came about, and mum, dad, grandparents, aunts, uncles, you name it - everybody came!"*

In the years that followed, Nottingham and Bradford Melas realised there was a scarcity of qawwali ensembles in Britain. While organisers were spoilt for choice in terms of vibrant bhangra groups, the shortage of qawwali made it difficult to balance the music programme. Champak Kumar of Oriental Arts remembers one Bradford based group enjoying the monopoly. *"I think qawwali is still a specialist form and you've got to have this formal vocal chord training. With bhangra, it's only the big people like Channi and Malkit and Safri, they have been trained in India. And with qawwali I think you need good musicians but also a main vocalist who can sing good qawwalis. And then what about the people who are going to chorus with him! So I think nobody had that sort of training. So at the time Abdul Hamid & Party was the only group in the whole of the country and they used to tour around and I used to get bookings for them left, right and centre."*

Organisers sought innovative means to bring qawwali to their melas. Apna Arts developed links with a qawwali troupe in Pakistan, supplementing their performance at Nottingham Mela with a nationwide tour including an appearance at WOMAD, in order to make the venture cost effective. David Thomas remembers that Nottingham Mela even coordinated its dates to tie in with WOMAD to pick up qawwali acts that were programmed for the Festival: *"Around 2004/5, we had our Mela the weekend before or after the WOMAD Festival. We used to get in touch with WOMAD to see who was coming over because, every year, they seemed to have a qawwali band. Qawwali's just really difficult to get hold of. They're going to be expensive to bring over so they need to be over here, and sometimes the networks can be quite complex. Some independent promoters are really difficult to work with, so it's better to have an established organisation like WOMAD to work with. Basically we were seeing if we could take advantage of the qawwali band being over at that time. There might have been a promoter working with WOMAD to organise a short tour and we were in that right pocket of opportunity, that month."*

Nottingham Mela also showcased qawwali as a fusion between modern day qawwals and Fun-Da-Mental. Aki Nawaz says Fun-Da-Mental wanted to expose their sound to mela audiences, but they realised that their alternative stage presence, and perhaps reputation, could be off-putting to mela programmers: *"We wanted to play the melas so we'd give people an alternative. 'If you don't want Fun-Da-Mental on in its political form and all its madness, then let us do a collaboration with these qawwali singers'. When we did concerts with Aziz Mian or now Rizwan Moazzam or Javed Salamat, we'd first give respect and space to the tradition. We'd say, 'You go on first to do fifteen minutes of qawwali and then we'll come on. We'll fire up the machines and get the other instruments on board and you'll then work with our tracks'. Ours were obviously more groove based in terms of western music and what young people were used to. And the musicians would groove on top of our grooves, and it worked! So first we'd let people calm down, let people see the tradition, and then kind of blaspheme against the tradition but in a harmonious way, where people doing the tradition would actually enjoy what we were doing."*

## Emerging Sounds

Melas have a strong tradition of showcasing
emerging and experimental sounds. Skinder Hundal
from New Art Exchange explains that just as the
first melas in Bradford and Nottingham created a
vital opportunity for intercultural dialogue, these
events also generated a space for artists and
artforms to have new conversations. *"I remember
going to see Black Star Liner at the mela and
thinking, 'Well they haven't got much a crowd!'
because it was quite a new form of music, but they
were giving it their all. And I was listening to their
music and I was looking at the style of the singer
and it was something I'd never seen. And I
thought, 'This is fantastic that artists from the
South Asian community are trying out experimental
ways of expressing their music with western
sensibilities, and bringing them together to create
a new knowledge.' And I think that whole thing
around new knowledge is still current today. We
talk about intercultural dialogue now as opposed
to multiculturalism, but artists were doing it twenty
years ago, you know exploring the notion of east
and west."*

**Fun-Da-Mental** | Nottingham Mela | 1992 | © Nadeem Haider/APNA Arts

Sukhy Johal MBE, is Vice Chair of New Art Exchange and former Chair of Apna Arts. He believes that since the melas appealed to a broad cross section of the Asian community – different faiths and ethnicities, youth and family, bhangra lovers and ghazal fans - they were perfectly placed to bring emerging sounds to a new critical mass. *"When you look through those early artists from Apache Indian to Johnny Zee, we had artists who broke down this notion of east and west. Their music was a fusion. It took the artform forward. Apache Indian was using styles from what would be related to African Caribbean communities, but relinked to inner cities where our Asian communities were growing, but there was still a desi vibe to them. And I was just thinking how we take it for granted now that there are artists like that. We weren't exposing these British based artists to a whole spectrum of audiences and ages and generations before, because those communities and age groups never came together. And that's probably the one thing that the mela has done – it's broken away from just having this community and that age group, but actually opening up to many different artforms from all over the subcontinent and UK British based artists to intergeneration – and that just didn't happen before. I think the mela was absolutely critical to exposing those kinds of artists to the communities and creating the critical mass of sales and exposure.*

While artists on stage were fusing eastern and western sounds, Asian youth off stage were feeling more confident about their cross cultural identities. Aki Nawaz reckons Fun-Da-Mental were regular fixtures at Nottingham Mela because their ethos chimed with the mission of Apna Arts to instil confidence in Asian youth: *"The people at Nottingham Mela were always progressive. They wanted a youth orientated vibe and I think that's what Fun-Da-Mental provided. We were about encouraging young people from our community to come out of their boxes and feel good. Just as they felt good about bhangra, we wanted them to feel that here was a band which was predominantly Asian representing them on more of an anarchic vibe. It was really important for me to influence young people into expressing themselves, being confident about what you are with all its chaos and confusion and these different cultures clashing, and to speak out. People like Parbinder were also interested in making our communities more confident, so they had a socialist outlook to their melas. The motives behind what Parbinder was doing were just a bit more than putting on a band. I'm saying that in a good way! They were on purpose using people like Fun-Da-Mental to express more of a resistant and militant thought process of their own. They'd put us on really late at night because they knew that all the aunties and uncles would have gone by then!"*

In recent years, melas have made more conscious efforts to represent the youth voice through emerging music scenes. Mela organisers also recognise the importance of programming the more popular sounds which mela audiences have come to expect. David Thomas, who has a particular interest in emerging sounds, programmed a youth arts mela just before the millennium. He explains that by strategically programming 'crowd pleasers' on the main stage, he was free to experiment elsewhere within the

Mela. He introduced sounds from the Asian underground in a specially erected black-out marquee. David recalls that the Asian underground at that time was facing some prejudice from mela programmers who didn't regard it as 'proper music': *"It took a long time for mela programmers to accept that if it wasn't a band, it was worthwhile. They were saying, 'If we're putting on high quality acts from India and Pakistan, and bhangra musicians who are playing their instruments, then to have people on the mics and MCs with backing tapes, then that's not proper music'. So we were the only mela programming any of the Asian underground. We brought in the Outcast Allstars, Black Star Liner, and Bobby Friction made his first ever appearance with us as a DJ. So there was quite a large experimental element. We just recognised that the young people's tastes were changing. There was a lot happening around the country where people were being experimental and as an arts organisation, we're always very keen to look at the cutting edge and new developments. We definitely had to make sure we brought in the crowd pullers - so we had Stereo Nation and Malkit Singh playing, but hopefully giving them an opportunity to see new talent."*

As Bradford Mela's music specialist Katherine Canoville explains, Bradford Mela's dedicated area for programming experimental sounds is a huge hit with young people. *"The whole idea of the Guava Stage was to be very experimental and stick things back to back that you might not ordinarily see. It's to create a platform where people can play around with music. We looked at putting in some DJ type things, some fusion things, and not so much of the traditional anything really. It is the younger element that are looking to stretch Asha Bhosle, to hear Asha Bhosle with Drum and Bass. They're open to listening to what's in their face on a day to day basis – pop music – but with what they already know which is their own cultural music. I think they're enjoying marrying the two, and it does seem to work really well."*

The mela clearly plays an important role in developing new audiences for music artists, but perhaps the role is even more significant for artists that attract a strong youth following. Mira Kaushik is Artistic Director of Akademi Dance. She believes that working the mela circuit can significantly increase an artist's fan base and popularity. Her teenage daughter went from one mela to the next throughout the summer months with her friends, following Jay Sean. *"My daughter was part of the thirteen year-old girls camp who started promoting Jay Sean in their network. This is five or six years ago before Facebook started. These groupies texted each other where Jay Sean was performing, and they travelled to every possible mela around the South of England at least. They hung around the mela circuit because it was free and accessible. She was not allowed to go to adult places but the mela was outdoors and it was daytime, all of that. That is really where most of the upcoming artists start with the thirteen year-olds following, the ones that go for everything which is new. These kids have now grown out of those mela circuits and have created the market as buyers of CDs and therefore they are the ones who have made these people saleable. So I would say melas have a huge huge role in mainstreaming of South Asian artists by giving them a business platform to promote themselves. If you do a local free gig in a mela, it's like a sample experience for the local community, and then on the back of it a lot of things can happen. And Jay Sean still hasn't returned to his dentistry course which he left!"*

As she points out, Mira deemed melas to be acceptable territory for her young daughter for a number of reasons: they were held at weekends so attendance didn't eat into school time; as free events, they were affordable for a group of teenage girls; they were held outdoors so perceived to be a more appropriate environment to an indoor venue like a club; and the long summer evenings added to the sense of safety.

Alaap performed at the first Bradford Festival in 1987 – the year before Bradford Mela was launched. Alaap also performed during Bradford Mela's twenty-one year celebrations in 2009. This time though, Channi Singh appeared with his daughter, Mona Singh. He believes melas are invaluable for generating publicity. While his appearance at Bradford Mela's milestone will help to keep him in the public eye, Mona was able to boost her fan base – according to Channi Singh, she performed at 90% of British melas during 2008.

**Jay Sean** | Nottingham Mela | 2006 | © Alan Lodge

# Reinventing the Mela

More than two decades after Bradford and
Nottingham Melas started, they have emerged as
major players within the arts industry in Britain.
Although their journeys began as celebrations of
South Asian culture, they are now recognised
internationally as cutting edge multi-arts festivals.
Melas now draw huge audiences from diverse
communities. Audience research at the 2009
Bradford Mela suggests that around 50% of the
200,000 visitors over the two day event were
non-Asians. Yet, melas are still perceived to be
Asian events catering for the South Asian
community. As they come of age, one of the
greatest obstacles for melas is to challenge these
perceptions.

African drumming workshop for families | Bradford Mela | 2005 | © Tim Smith

One of mela's achievements must be its ability to skilfully reflect contemporary debate around issues of identity and heritage, through a variety of emerging arts and soundscapes. Skinder Hundal believes that mela is still playing this role as its audiences grapple with fresh global challenges. *"With bands like Black Star Liner, it was about the role mela played in shaping people's identities and connections with their heritage, but also exploring where we were going as a community. And bands like Fun-Da-Mental who were quite political were actually creating a consciousness at the time about who we are and what we're facing. And people like Aki Nawaz are still at the forefront of that debate. They're still coming back into the fold to respond to situations that we're facing in the country at the moment post 9/11 and 7/7, so those issues around alienation for the community are still relevant today. And I think what's interesting is that the Mela explores these issues in a soft way by using arts and music and it creates a dialogue. Sometimes it's unconscious and sometimes it's conscious and I think it's an alternative way of exploring identity and politics as well and just enjoying the beauty of art."*

The barrier to participation for some begins with the word 'mela' and its South Asian origins. The Oxford English Dictionary defines 'mela' as "a fair or Hindu festival, originated from the Sanskrit 'mela' assembly". Although mela is widely interpreted in British terms as a celebratory gathering, its South Asian roots can, unhelpfully, imbue the word with religious or cultural associations. Liam Sinclair, Artistic Director of Edinburgh Mela recalls a speech by the Lord Provost of Edinburgh at the opening of the 2007 Edinburgh Mela, when he

related the word 'mela' to the Gaelic term 'ceilidh': *"Everyone thinks of ceilidh in terms of Scottish dancing, but what it means is gathering. That might be sitting round, having a cup of tea and a blather or it might be a bigger event."* The point he was making was in cultures across the world, people have always gathered in order to socialise and celebrate. It's that universal nature of what mela means. In that kind of light, it would almost be a shame to lose the word.

The dawn of Bradford and Nottingham Melas coincided with the golden era of British bhangra music. It is now the children of artists that headlined Bhangra Heatwave and brought the Bradford Mela to a close on the Stage on the Lake, that dominate the modern bhangra movement. So bhangra remains an important force in the contemporary mela and particularly music oriented melas like Cardiff. In Bradford and Nottingham, the likes of H-Dhami and Mona Singh are programmed within the context of a variety of music genres and artforms. In spite of this though, melas are still strongly identified with bhangra. Rajinder Dudrah is author of Bhangra – Birmingham and Beyond. He suggests this perception could simply be down to the critical role that bhangra music played during the melas of the eighties and early nineties. *"Maybe it's something that lingers on from the old days, maybe because bhangra was so core to the mela. For those people who were really into their British Asian identity and were political or politicised in that way, bhangra was a music to announce, 'We're loud and proud, and this is our rock and pop'. And what we're seeing now is that the British Asian music scene has diversified a lot. But in terms of why people are still thinking that,* then I think it probably is a hangover of the old heydays of the live bhangra music scene."

Sheena Wrigley oversaw the running of the Mela when she was employed by Bradford Council as Head of Bradford Theatres, Arts and Festivals from 2003-2007. She says she worked hard to illustrate that the Mela is no longer an exclusively Asian event and that everyone is welcome. *"We used to look very carefully at what images we picked to use on posters, to use on press releases, to use on our website, always making sure that we were projecting an inclusive and exciting image with different generations, different groupings of people so it didn't just look like an Asian youth music event."* However, Sheena feels frustrated by the simplicity with which Bradford is reflected in the media, locally and nationally. Little attempt is made to reflect Bradford's diversity in its true sense, which in turn creates a misconception of Bradford and its Mela audience: *"If you looked at the audience data, certainly for the period I was involved, there was a pretty high percentage of non-Asian attenders but it was almost impossible to communicate that strongly enough. There was one particular year where the Telegraph and Argus did a lovely double page photo-spread and every shot that they used was of typical young Asian men, you know really getting on a high in front of the main stage, missing so much of the other elements of the event. And I walked round with this photographer and I know she came on a day when there was a high percentage of non-Asian attenders, but none of that was shown. I think they genuinely thought that they were demonstrating a reality of the event but I don't think it was. The way the press wrote about it in particular, and*

*constantly inferred through images, just reinforced the sense people had that perhaps it wasn't an event for them."*

Critically, misreading the personality of mela in this way can jeopardise its potential to attract funding. Mela may not be deemed eligible for 'mainstream' funding; instead, funds earmarked to boost agendas such as community cohesion may be regarded as more appropriate. This risks stereotyping mela as little more than a tokenistic showcase for minorities, making it a pawn in local authority agendas. Moreover, the mela's potential for boosting the local economy is completely undermined. It is for precisely these reasons that events like melas are targeted by right wing groups. For example, the BNP posted leaflets in the neighbourhood around the Bradford Mela site in 2007, suggesting that money spent on melas should be diverted into events like St. George's Day parades.

Zulfi Karim is a Cultural Strategy and Major Events Specialist who helped to bring the Bollywood Oscars (International Indian Film Academy Awards) to Yorkshire in 2007. He says it is time for melas to make a business case. He believes that when melas first started, their economic impact could not justify a business case: *"Twenty years ago melas were nice because they celebrated a minority community and what it had to offer to the city. Therefore the business case was never there. The investment was there from a community angle but the business case was never strong enough. But as melas grew and the numbers grew, from 10,000 to 100,000 plus, now there's a critical mass there. And the critical mass has a huge effect on the* economics. So economically the mela is far stronger than it was twenty years ago, but the economic case has never been fought for."

It may be the case that mela organisers deferred making the business case because they felt ill equipped to do so. Bradford Mela Producer, Ben Pugh believes that the sector now recognises that business acumen and creativity need to go hand in hand for survival. *"Nowadays there are more and more people doing management or business type training that are in the cultural industries and the arts, because they recognise that you have to be able to manage limited resources in an effective manner to be able to deliver the creative objectives that you're working towards." Ben also agrees that there is now a business case to be made: "We know from our independent evaluation that the Bradford Mela generates over £7million worth of spend. When you look at that, and you look at the positive impact on economic indicators and the impact on tourism and profile and community cohesion and safer stronger communities, Bradford Mela ticks off against corporate priorities across the board."*

Before the business case is fought, melas face the challenge of shifting stereotypes which have become deep seated throughout their twenty-one year relationship with local authorities. Encouraging them to focus on the true value of mela would require a dramatic shift in the event's relationship with the local authorities, as Ben Pugh explains: *"Being so well supported by Bradford Council has allowed for a period of growth and relative stability, but the problem that comes from a deep affiliation with a local authority is that the*

*business case is simply about bottom line. It's not even really about what the measurable outputs are. It's simply about, 'Is there enough money in the budget to put it on this year?' The question should be, can you afford not to do it? Is there anything else that you can do which so coherently builds and develops and manages at such a wide range of intangible measurable?"*

Melas need to engage in a similar dialogue with arts development agencies which have yet to truly recognise the mela's potential as a major, cutting edge multi-arts festival, delivering high quality innovative work. As Nottingham and Bradford Melas mark their coming of age, their challenge is to position themselves as agents of change to ensure their recognition is appropriate to their achievements. Ben Pugh, Producer of Bradford Mela reflects: *"If there is one key thing that we can learn from the last twenty-one years, it would be the importance of the principle, 'Why we do this, has to be the foundation for how we do this'. The Mela for me is so much about the beauty that comes from the sum of its parts. If we are celebrating the culture, creativity and communities of our district then we have to be open to what people want to bring – and recognise the tremendous value they bring along with their ideas and input. We need to find the best ways of supporting and facilitating the widest range of partners and stakeholders, and in that way the Mela will keep reinventing itself. It will keep being fresh and engaging and keep being true to its roots, its vision and the communities it is shared by."*

**A boy making his way home through Lister Park** | Bradford Mela | 1991 | © Tim Smith

# Acknowledgements

Key workers within the Nottingham and Bradford Mela have had a long history of friendly rivalry, teasing each other about who was the first National Mela in the UK. It was during one of these ongoing disputes between Champak Kumar and myself over a few Kingfishers in Mumbai, that Alan Tweedie suggested both organisations get together and celebrate 21 years of mela. The next day, my mind buzzing with ideas, I saw a poster celebrating the achievement of a local Indian business. The strap-line stated: *"Some people think we have gone a long way, we think it is just the beginning"*.

These events ignited a spark. I subsequently arranged a meeting between both Nottingham and Bradford Mela, and three years later, with a touring exhibition, book, website and oral history project behind us, I am very pleased and proud to be part of this important milestone within the history of the mela.

I would like to thank: Alan Tweedie for first igniting this idea; Mandeep Samra for coordinating the project and making it such a smooth journey; Harmeet Sembi for his creative input as the designer; Ben Pugh, Champak Kumar, Skinder Hundal and Bhavesh Jani for their support, advice and direction; and all the volunteers including Roshni Belakavadi, Tom Hodgson, Shabana Kausar, Pavan Sembi and Lu Li, who have worked so professionally on this project.

I am also grateful to the writer Irna Qureshi, for providing a balanced, informative and hugely readable text for the book; Steve Dearden for editing the text; and all the photographers/organisations who have supplied some quality images for this project; Tim Smith, Nadeem Haider/APNA Arts, Alan Lodge, Bartosz Kali, Jagdish Patel/Frontline Images, Ashok Mistry, ArtReach and JMS Photography.

On a personal basis I would also like to thank the pioneers and volunteers of the early Nottingham and Bradford Mela, whose dedication and vision ignited the spark over 21 years ago, and who have made working in the environment memorable and fun. Thank you to Parbinder Singh, Sukhy Johal, Nadeem Haider, Mohan Khera (amongst others) from Nottingham Mela. Also thank you to Dusty Rhodes, Allan Brack, and Champak Kumar from Bradford Mela.

Lastly, and most importantly, I would like to thank the Heritage Lottery Fund for their financial and moral support, and especially lead officer Louise Clare.

**David Schischka Thomas**